An Introduction to the Gift of Living in the Divine Will

DEREK WILLIAMS

* * * * *

Verbum
Publications

Published by: *Verbum Publications*
www.verbumpublications.com
ISBN: 978-1-0687739-3-8

First published 2024
Printed in The United Kingdom

Acknowledgments

'I thank my God always concerning you for the grace of God which was given you in Christ Jesus.'

1 Corinthians 1:4

I thank God for the great grace of living in His Divine Will, the greatest heavenly treasure.

My gratitude to my wife Lynn who proposed a few amendments and proofread my manuscript. I always thank my children, Sr Caty, Michael, Hannah, Sam, who are a great support to my work in evangelisation.

Thank you to my impromptu team of proofreaders: Annelies Clovis, Marie Lienard-Yeterian, Fr Dominic O'Connor, Brunella McMahon, who also proposed a few amendments to the manuscript and gave me some cultural insights for Luisa's situation in life (thank Bru).

My thanks to Tom Goymour for lots of helpful advice regarding publishing, both hard copies and e-copies. The help and guidance is always invaluable.

Thank you to Nick Clovis for the outstanding cover art, and his friendship over the years in the Divine Will.

Thank you to St Joseph the Worker who stands over my laptop helping me to focus on the task in hand and repeatedly tells me:

If you get down to work, all your difficulties will disappear, and will fall off like fish scales. [1]

Finally, thank you to Mother Mary, the Queen of the Kingdom of the Divine Will to whom this book is consecrated. She comes to the assistance of all who ask for her help. She encourages us with her beautiful words:

I come to invite you to enter the Kingdom of your tender mother – the Kingdom of the Divine Will – and I knock at the door of your heart that you may invite me in. You know it is with my own hands that I bring you this book as a gift. I offer it to you with my maternal care so that, in reading it, you in turn may learn to live by the life of heaven and no longer by that of earth. [2]

Fiat!

---

[1] Piccarreta, L., Book of Heaven, Volume 5, March 20th, 1903.
[2] Piccarreta, L. The Blessed Virgin Mary in the Kingdom of the Divine Will.

Contents

Introduction

'You have saved the best wine until last.'

John 2:10

The journey you have begun into God's Divine Will is the greatest journey of your life and if you persevere it will continue for all eternity. The teaching you have started receiving is the richest, purest, and most wonderful that you will ever hear. It is the science of sciences, the sanctity of sanctities, and the purest gold which will radically transform your interior life.

This teaching comes from the pen of the Italian mystic Luisa Piccarreta. She received it all from Christ and wrote numerous books in obedience to Him and the Church appointed spiritual directors that she had. I will refer to Luisa throughout this book and mainly her 36 volume work the title of which came from the Lord Jesus Christ in a vision:

"The Kingdom of my Divine Will in the midst of creatures. Book of Heaven. The call of the creature to the order, the place and the purpose for which he was created by God."[3]

---

[3] Piccarreta, L., Book of Heaven, Volume 19, August 27th, 1926.

The first chapter is a prayerful introduction which will prepare your heart for the teachings that follow, and each chapter explains a different aspect of this beautiful gift. However, this is a very basic introduction. Luisa wrote 36 volumes, plus several other books all of which were a result of communications from Jesus or Our Lady. So there is a vast amount that is not included in this book, which is the nature of an introductory work.

The chapter about Luisa is at the end of this book. This is done deliberately: during her life on earth Luisa wanted to be hidden and silent, she did not want to be known to anybody but her Lord and Saviour Jesus Christ, so I have hidden her at the back. That also means that the introduction to her writings is focussed on the teaching rather than the person, even though the person of Luisa is going to be very instrumental in your life if you persevere with this work.

Finally, you have been chosen for this beautiful gift. Jesus has longed to give this to you for thousands of years. At last he can fuse it into your soul with your cooperation and then teach you about it. He is the teacher of the Divine Will, and the only one who teaches with authority (Matthew 7:29). In His own words:

"Finally, after six thousand years you have come back. You have gone wandering, you have experienced all evils, because there is no good without Our Fiat. You have experienced enough, and have touched with your own hand what it means to go out of It; so, never go out of It

again, and come to rest and enjoy what is yours, because in Our Volition everything was given to you."

Jesus to Luisa, April 28th, 1929.

Fiat!

A Personal Witness

'They have conquered him by the blood of the Lamb and by the word of their testimony.'

Revelation 12:11

By 2010 I had been working in evangelisation for 20 years, sometimes full time, but not always, some were part time – that year was full time. A friend gave me a prophetic word telling me that God wanted me to deliver retreats in Spain. I contacted a few friends and found a retreat centre in Garabandal called 'The House of Sanctification.' I asked the owners if I could run a retreat there, they said 'no', but welcomed me to give some teaching on a retreat of theirs that was coming up. That retreat began shortly after Easter 2010. The retreat was about The Gift of Living in the Divine Will in the writings of the Servant of God, Luisa Piccarreta, but at the time I knew nothing about this doctrine. I planned to give some teachings on the Sabbath rest.

The first few days of the retreat were incredibly difficult for me. I knew that what was being taught was incredible, and I found corresponding references to all of the teachings in the Bible that I had on my lap throughout the retreat. It was just a purgative experience. After a few days I rang my wife and told her of my struggle. Her response, 'Derek, Our Lady wants you there, just try and receive what she is offering you.' As she spoke these words it was like a light poured down from above and flooded my soul. After this, everything made sense, the retreat became electrifying, and I received all of the beautiful teaching that was being offered.

Shortly after coming back my father passed away, and then I was taken out of action by severe sciatica, an inflammation of the nerve at the base of the spine which can be very painful. I reveal this because the journey into the Divine Will goes by way of the cross, as does any serious journey towards union with God. The roses have all got thorns. The sciatica was excruciating, and I could only get relief by lying on the floor. I did not have the faith to believe I could be healed, that is, until Our Lady granted me a special grace.

The feast of the Assumption, August 15th 2010: My wife had taken our four young children to Mass and I was lying on the lounge floor. I asked Our Lady if she would touch my sciatica nerve. I knew that if she touched it, on her feast day, it would be immediately healed. 'Just one touch from the Queen changes everything.'[4] That was all that was needed. I lay there asking her to touch the nerve for a little while when suddenly all of the pain vanished – just like that! I did some stretching, flexing, standing, moving about. No pain – nothing. It had completely gone. This little cross and miracle were a part of my journey into the Divine Will. After this happened, on the feast of the Assumption, which

[4] A subtle change in the lyrics to a Godfrey Birtills hymn, 'Just one touch from the King changes everything.'

Jesus reveals in his teachings to Luisa Piccarreta, will be the feast of the Divine Will, I started reading more and more of the Divine Will writings and introducing my family into this beautiful treasure.

I continued my evangelisation work until another cross manifested itself in July 2015. I was jogging with my dog early in the morning and he ran across my path. I flipped over him, and landed upside down, heavily on my back. My rib cage shattered and separated a little from the rest of my skeleton, moving about quite freely. My entire chest area was loose. I contacted the hospital but they could not treat it and told me all I could do was rest.

A few weeks after this, my wife and I went to the New Dawn conference, which was our annual pilgrimage with the children, camping for the week, yes, even with a shattered rib cage. All went well until the Thursday night. There was a special prayer meeting at the conference and attendees were encouraged to come to the front for prayer ministry. This is when I received another prophetic word from a friend who was praying over me (laying on of hands). As she prayed with her hand on my shoulder, she had a vision in her imagination of a road ahead of me, and the road was taking a sharp turn. She said that she believed the Lord was speaking to me through this image, and He was telling me that my life was about to take an unexpected turn.

A few hours later I woke up in the middle of the night in agony and had to be taken into hospital. I stayed there a few days undergoing tests but was sent home and I was told to rest – no work. A few days later, just before my 50th birthday, a friend sent me a collection of Divine Will material to read. My daughter Hannah said, 'Dad, you are not listening to Jesus, you need to pay more attention to what he is saying.' I started studying the Divine Will material more assiduously believing that this was part of the 'turn in the road' that had been revealed to me the previous week.

A month or so later I was at an evangelisation event in the south of England, my first speaking event since my injury. A friend met me after I had spoken, she was looking to buy a house near the National Catholic Shrine of Our Lady of Walsingham and wanted it to be for an evangelist. I explained that we were having to sell our house due to my accident and the subsequent fall in income, and perhaps God wanted us to move there. Within six months she had purchased the house for us to rent and we moved, in May 2016. This was part of the 'unexpected change in direction' that had been part of that vision. It is to be noted that throughout this time I was studying the writings that I am going to share with you in this book.

I continued my evangelisation work into 2016, but it was clear Our Lady was asking me to lay it all down and take something of a sabbatical. This had been hinted at by my spiritual director and my wife, Lynn. I wasn't getting any invitations to give parish retreats, speak at conferences, or speak at seminars, but I had been offered a full-time position at the Shrine of Our Lady of Walsingham which was just a mile from where we lived. Consequently, on the feast of Our Lady of Walsingham in 2016 I did my last speaking event for the year and the following day my manager at the Shrine, gave me all of Luisa Piccarreta's diaries (which are what this book is an introduction to – the Gift of Living in the Divine Will,) and told me to read them on my sabbatical. The broken rib cage led to a sabbatical during which I would be studying Luisa's writings. This was confirmed both by my wife and my spiritual director.

My sabbatical eventually lasted six years! In June 2022, after a very painful and testing time of confusion, (more crosses) it was made clear to me that I had to give up my position at the Shrine where I had become a Sacristan, and get back into full time evangelisation, particularly, giving Divine Will retreats. This was from both my spiritual director and my wife. I did not see this coming. In June 2022 I resigned from my position at the Shrine, and in November of that year I received a text message from a Romanian Divine Will leader asking if I could give a retreat there. The retreat was just over a week away and had been requested by the Archbishop of Bucharest.

God placed everything in my path and drew me in an unexpected direction. I quote two of my favourite scriptures:

'I will lead the blind in a way they do not know.'

Isaiah 42:16

And again:

'And your ears shall hear a word behind you, saying, "This is the way, walk in it," when you turn to the right or when you turn to the left.'

Isaiah 30:21

I had no idea that God was going to lead me on this path and unfold the infinitely rich treasures of His Divine Will to me. It has been a breathtaking journey of discovery, Divine revelation, with many crosses.

Consequently, I encourage you to open wide your heart to the infinitely rich graces that God wishes to pour into your soul through this most incredible science, the science of sciences, the science of the interior life of God. In the words of Pope St John Paul 2 on the occasion of his being elected Pope:

'Do not be afraid to welcome Christ and accept his power. …Do not be afraid. Open wide the doors for Christ.'

My wife and I will be praying for you as you move forward on this journey. Indeed, all of the children of the Divine Will are praying for people to receive this beautiful gift, so you have a global community praying for you.

Fiat!

1. The Prelude to the Teachings

'I have given them the words which you gave me, and they received them.'

John 17:8

'I begin. With a Novena of Holy Christmas'

Volume 1[5]

Jesus gave Luisa the nine excesses of love to Luisa when she was aged seventeen as a prelude to his teachings on the Divine Will. Consequently, it is logical that if we meditate on these nine excesses first, they will help dispose our soul for the blazing light of the Divine Will teachings, which will follow them. After each of the nine excesses spend a few moments contemplating each of the mysteries and follow the guidance given.

What is a prelude?

The concept of prelude belongs to music but also to rhetoric, the art of persuasion, and expresses the need to introduce, to predict or preannounce what will follow immediately afterwards. It is an elegant, imaginative and

[5] Piccarreta, L., Nine Excesses of Love, Divine Will Prayer Book, translated by Fr Joseph Iannuzzi. Missionaries of the Holy Trinity.

improvisational gesture, capable of predisposing the minds of the bystanders by stimulating their attention. Think about the great classical operas! Is there anything more peaceful than the prelude to La Traviata? The dictionary definition is of a "free form" instrumental piece with an introductory character that precedes an operatic act. Consider this chapter as the 'free form' instrumental piece that introduces the great opera of the Divine Will. It is a meditation on the time when Jesus was in Mary's womb, from his perspective, and the graces he wants to grant to you in order that you are correctly disposed to receiving the gift of living in the Divine Will. The nine excesses are the introductory melody.

"These nine excesses of my love, manifested with so much love of tenderness and simplicity, formed the prelude of the many lessons I was to give you about my Divine Fiat, in order to form Its Kingdom. And now, by their being read, my love is renewed and redoubled. Don't you want, then, that my love, being redoubled, overflow outside and invest more hearts, so that, as a prelude, they may dispose themselves for the lessons of my Will, to make It known and reign?"

Volume 25, December 16th 1928.

The First Excess of Love [of the Most Holy Trinity]

To offer an example, with my mind I brought myself to Paradise for one hour, and with my imagination envisioned the Most Holy Trinity:

The Father sending the Son to earth; the Son promptly obeying the Father's Will, and the Holy Spirit consenting to the Son's Incarnation.

In contemplating such a great mystery my mind was perplexed: For I beheld a love so requiting, so consistent and so powerful among the three of them and toward mankind that I was overwhelmed. Then, I beheld the ingratitude of men, and especially of my own country. I would have remained there not for one hour, but for the whole day, but an interior voice told me: "This is enough for now. Come and behold other greater excesses of My love."

This first excess draws us into contemplation of the love exchanged within the Blessed Trinity using the faculty of our imagination. It offers us two things to contemplate. Firstly, the love and unity of the Blessed Trinity. Secondly, the ingratitude of men. Consider the ardent love of the Father who wants to save His most beloved creature[6] from the disorders caused by his human will and bring him back to his original essence, 'the order, the place and the purpose for which he was created by God.' He wanted to accomplish this by the incarnation on earth of the Eternal Word.

Contemplate the ardent exchanging love of the Son, the Eternal Word who obeys the will of the Father, and desired to be exiled by coming down on earth to live and take upon Himself the Divine justice. He experienced our pain and suffering caused by our disobedience, and by His infinite mercy, redeemed us. Consider the love of the Holy Spirit

---

6 singular because Jesus says all human family is seen as one Vol 25-17 Dec 25 1928

who wants to give the total and infinite Divine dimensions to all the acts of sanctification, redemption and glory of the incarnate Word, which we are asked to take part in by living in the Divine Will.

The Second Excess of Love [of the Son of God]

Then, my mind brought itself into the Virgin Mary's womb, and in considering Jesus, I was left completely speechless upon beholding a God so great in heaven, and yet now so utterly helpless, restricted and constrained that He hasn't the ability to so much as move or where he can barely breathe.

The interior voice then said to me: "Do you see how much I have loved you? Oh please, make a little space for Me in your heart; remove from yourself all that which opposes Me and, in this way, you will allow Me to breathe and move more freely in My mother's womb."

With my heart enflamed I asked Jesus' forgiveness, and promised him that I would give myself completely over to him. I wept profusely, but – I say this to my embarrassment – I would then go back to behaving as I did with my usual defects. O Jesus, how good you are with this wretched soul!

In this excess of love, Jesus specifically asks us to make room for Him in our hearts. The Lord is going to offer your soul the greatest treasure in Heaven, the gift of living in the Divine Will. Consequently, He needs you to make room in your heart for such a great grace. This requires a purging on our part. Examine your heart, consider the things in life that you are unhealthily attached to, and ask the Lord for the grace to be detached from these things. It does not mean you have to throw out your possessions, money, etc. It means to be detached from them even if you have them in your possession. On the other hand, God may invite you to have a little 'clear out' of some goods that you might not have used in a long time.

"My daughter, the best way to make Me be born in one's own heart, is to empty oneself of everything, because in finding empty space, I can place all my goods in it. And only then can I remain in it forever, if there is room to be able to carry all that belongs to Me, all that is my own. A person who went to live in the house of someone else, could be called happy only if he found empty space in which to be able to put all of his belongings; otherwise, he would be unhappy. So I am". [7]

To conclude this excess, offer your heart to Jesus in prayer and you will be ready for the next excess:

'Jesus, I offer you my heart and ask for the grace to give myself completely to you – Lord, give me the grace to remove from myself all that which opposes you.'

Third Excess of Love [of the Son of God]

As I proceeded from the second to the third meditation, an interior voice said to me:

---

[7] Piccarreta, L. Book of Heaven, Volume 8, December 25th 1908.

"My child, place your head upon the womb of My mother, peer deep within and behold My little humanity. My love devoured Me: My divine flames, divine oceans and divinely immense seas of love inundated Me, completely consumed Me and unleashed flames that were so high that they overwhelmed and enveloped everyone – all human generations, from the first to the last man. My little humanity was devoured by My divine flames.

Compelled as I was by the divine flames of My eternal love, do you know what it is that I set ablaze? Ah, souls! I was satisfied only after I had conceived all souls within [Me at the moment of] My Conception and enveloped them in My divine flames of love. I was God, and if I was to operate as God, I had to set all souls ablaze. My love would have afforded Me no peace had I excluded so much as one soul. Ah My daughter, peer well into the womb of My mother, fix well your eyes on My conceived humanity, and you will find your soul conceived within Me and the flames of My love enveloping you. Oh, how much I loved you, and love you still!"

I was completely overwhelmed in the face of so much love, and unable to detach myself from it, when a voice called me loudly, saying: "My daughter, this is nothing; cleave to Me more tightly and give your hands to My dear mother so that she may press you to her motherly womb. Behold anew My little humanity that has just been conceived, and behold the fourth excess of My love."

Jesus wants to set all souls ablaze, and this means you. He invites you to fix your gaze on His humanity, which is the equivalent of inviting you to contemplate His humanity. One way to do this is to gaze on an image of the Divine

Mercy, the Sacred Heart, a crucifix, or some other physical image of the Lord. Alternatively, try to imagine Jesus in the womb, constrained and in the dark, unable to move because we are not giving Him room and gaze on that image for a while. By doing this, Jesus explains that He can set your soul ablaze which is part of the preparation for the great treasure He wishes to impart to your soul. One would think that the soul being ablaze is going to be the great gift, but He has so much more to give you. Note His words to you, 'This is nothing…' There is always so much more that God wants us to have from His hands. This is God's masterpiece of salvation, in the womb of Mary, there is not only Jesus, but in her womb, we were also created sons of God and brothers of Christ.

…in the same way, these gigantic waves of flames which rose from these seas of fire, by devouring the creatures, wanted to be the life, the guide, the defense, the food, the bed, the palace, the fatherland of creatures. But as they go out of this sea of love, all of a sudden, they find death. And little Baby Jesus cries, moans, prays, shouts and sighs, for He wants no one to go out of these devouring flames of His, because He does not want to see anyone die. [8]

'I knew you before I formed you in your mother's womb. Before you were born, I set you apart.'

Jeremiah 1:5

---

[8] Piccarreta, L. Book of Heaven, volume 25, Dec 21st 1928.

Fourth Excess of Love [of the Son of God]

"My child, now that you have contemplated My devouring love, behold My operating love. Each soul that I conceived within My Conception brought me the burden of its sins, its weakness and its passions, whence My love compelled me to take up the burden of each one of them. My love conceived not only souls, but the sorrows of each soul, as well as the satisfaction each soul is [required] to offer My Heavenly Father. So My Passion was conceived along with My humanity. Fix your eyes well on Me in the womb of My Heavenly Mother.

Oh how tortured My little humanity is; take a good look at My little head, surrounded with a crown of thorns which, pressed tightly around my temples, made rivers of tears pour out from My eyes; I am unable to move in the slightest way to dry them. O Please, unite yourself to My Passion; you, whose arms are free, dry My eyes from so much crying. These thorns are the crown of the many evil thoughts that fill human minds. Oh, how they pierce Me more than the thorns the earth produces.

Oh, behold the long crucifixion of nine months in which I can move neither My hands nor feet; I cannot so much as move a finger. I remain continuously immobile, as there isn't any room for Me to make the slightest motion. What a long and hard crucifixion. What is more, there [here with Me] are all the evil works of souls that assume the form of nails which continuously pierced My hands and feet."

Jesus continued to narrate one sorrow after another – all the martyrdoms of his little humanity were so many that if I wanted to tell them all, it would take too long. Whence I burst into tears, and heard in my interior:

"My daughter, I wish to hug you, but am unable to do so, as there is no room for Me to move; My immobility restrains Me from doing so. I want to approach you, but I am unable to walk. For now, you may approach Me and hug Me. Later, when I emerge from My mother's womb, I will approach you".

But as I hugged Him and pressed Him tightly to my heart with my imagination, an interior voice told me: "This is enough for now, My child. Proceed to consider the fifth excess of My love."

In this excess of love, Jesus distinguishes between His devouring love and His operating love. The former is the flames of love that devoured Him, and with which He wants to devour us. The latter, the operating love, is His sufferings through which He redeems us, saves us, and can raise us up to the eternal mode of prayer and action that is the gift of living in the Divine Will.[9] He explains to us that during His time in the womb, from His conception to His birth, He suffered a long crucifixion. During this time of suffering He invites us to 'bilocate' through the use of our imagination into the womb of the Blessed Virgin Mary, to approach Him, hug Him and dry the tears from His eyes because He is unable to move. We can be His hands that dry His eyes, give Him comfort and console Him from the pain caused by human thoughts that are sharp like thorns around His head.

---

[9] Eternal mode of prayer and action - to be explained in subsequent chapters.

In this dark prison we can make our voice ring out and say to Him 'I Love you, I adore you, I bless you.' This will console Jesus and bring many graces to your soul. Spend a few moments doing this now!

Fifth Excess of Love [of the Son of God]

The interior voice continued: "My child, do not distance yourself from Me; do not leave Me alone. My love seeks your company. This is yet another excess of My love: In not wanting to be alone, do you know whose company it is that I seek? I seek the [company of the] soul's love. Behold all souls along with Me in the womb of My mother – conceived together with Me – and I am here for them in the form of pure love. I wish to tell them how much I love them; I wish to speak with them, to tell them of My joys and sorrows.

I wish to tell them how I have come to dwell with them to console them and make them happy; that I will remain with each and every one of them as their little brother to convey to them at the cost of My life, all of My blessings and My Kingdom. I wish to offer them My kisses and My loving finesses. I wish to delight in them. But, alas, how many sorrows they cause Me! Some flee from Me, while others play deaf and force Me into silence; some despise My blessings and care not of My Kingdom, while others requite My kisses and loving finesses with indifference, and become completely estranged to Me. This is how souls change My playful invitation into bitter tears. Though I am among so many, oh how lonely I am; oh, how much this loneliness weighs upon Me.

I have no one with whom to share one word, with whom to pour Myself out, not even in love. I remain continuously downcast, without anyone with whom to speak, for if I do speak, I am ignored. Alas My daughter, I beg you, I implore you, do not leave Me alone in such utter loneliness. Grant Me the pleasure of allowing Me to speak by listening to Me; lend your ears to My teachings. I am the Master of masters. How many things I wish to teach you! If you only listen closely to what your tender mother wishes to tell you,[10] you will stop My crying, and I will rejoice in you. Do you not wish for Me to rejoice in you?"

As I abandoned myself in Jesus, uniting myself to His Passion in His state of loneliness, the interior voice continued: "Enough, enough for now. Proceed to consider the sixth excess of My love."

Jesus calls us to draw closer to Him in love. He desires your love, no matter how poor and weak you think your love may be. In prayer offer Him your love and draw close to Him in the womb of the Blessed Virgin Mary. Jesus desires to speak with you and to shower your soul with loving kisses and other beautiful graces. All you need do is spend a few moments drawing close to Him as He was in the womb, and listen to His words. Then let those words penetrate the core of your being. Do as Luisa did in her final sentence; 'Jesus, I abandon myself in you and I unite myself to your passion'.

---

[10] There is a book titled 'The Blessed Virgin Mary in the Kingdom of the Divine Will' in which Our Lady gives us teachings on how to live this beautiful gift.

Then hear the voice of Jesus lovingly and longingly inviting you to the sixth excess of his love;

"Proceed to consider the sixth excess of my love."

Sixth Excess of Love [of the Son of God]

"My child, come and entreat My dear mother to set aside a little space for you within her motherly womb, so that you may see for yourself the sorrowful state in which I find myself".

And in my mind's eye, it seemed as if our Holy Queen Mother made a little room for me in order to make Jesus happy, and she placed me in her womb. But the darkness was so thick that I could not see Him. I could only hear His breathing, while He continued to say in my interior:

"My child, behold yet another excess of My love. I am eternal light. The sun is but a pale shadow of My light. And do you see where My love led me? Do you see in what a dark prison I am? There is not a glimmer of light; it is always night for Me, but a night without stars or rest, and I remain always awake... What pain! The narrow confines of this prison keep Me from making the slightest movement, they keep Me in thick darkness. Even My breathing is impaired, as I breathe through the breathing of My mother, and how laboured it is! And this is compounded by the darkness of the sins of souls. Each sin is a night for Me which, when joined together, form an abyss of darkness without boundaries. What pain! Oh the excess of My love: it compels Me to go from the immensity of light and space into an abyss of thick darkness

that is so narrow that I haven't the freedom to breathe – and all this, for love of souls."

As He was speaking, He moaned, but His moans were stifled because of the lack of space, and He wept. I was immersed in weeping. I thanked Him and offered Him my compassion. With my love I wanted to offer Him some light, as He had asked me to. But who can recount all that which had transpired? Then, the same interior voice added: "This is enough for now. Proceed to consider the seventh excess of My love."

Jesus invites you to ask Our Lady, the Queen of Peace, to make some room in her womb so that you may dwell alongside Him. He reveals to you that His time in the womb was in thick darkness, an abyss of obscurity without boundaries. A depth of deep darkness and so narrow to the point of not being able to breath freely. All of which He endured for us. However, by offering Him your love you can penetrate that darkness of sin with divine light. 'Jesus, with your Will, I love you.' this simple prayer brings the blazing light of the Divine Will into the womb of the Blessed Virgin Mary and consoles Jesus in his suffering.

Seventh Excess of Love [of the Son of God]

The interior voice continued: "My daughter, don't abandon Me amidst so much loneliness and in so much darkness; don't leave the womb of my mother. Remain and behold the seventh excess of My love.

In the womb of My Heavenly Father I enjoyed complete bliss – there was no blessing that I did not possess: Joy, enthrallments – everything was at My disposal. The angels adored Me reverently, hanging upon My every word. Oh, the excess of My love! I could say that such an excess made Me change my destiny: it led Me to the point of being restrained within this gloomy prison; it stripped Me of all My joys, bliss and blessings, and clothe Me with the whole gamut of soul's poor plight – and all this in order to requite souls by giving them My destiny, My joys and My eternal bliss.

But this would have been nothing if I did not find [and expiate] in souls their great ingratitude and obstinate betrayals. Oh, how shocked My eternal love was before so much ingratitude, and how I wept over mankind's callousness and betrayals. Ingratitude was the sharpest thorn to pierce My Heart from [the moment of] My Conception to the last moment of My life. Look at my little Heart: it is wounded and pours forth Blood. What pain! What torture I experience! My daughter, do not be ungrateful to Me. Ingratitude is the greatest sorrow for your Jesus – it is closing the door in My face and leaving Me outside numb in the cold. And yet, My love did not stop in the face of so much ingratitude, but assumed the role of interceding, imploring, moaning and begging for love, which forms the eighth excess of My love."

I remind you that these nine excesses of love are prayerful meditations that according to Jesus are the prelude to a more important work that He wants to do in your soul. You are cooperating with His grace and preparing yourself for the greatest of all heavenly treasures. You should be both excited and 'filled with expectation' (Luke 3:15). You are preparing your soul for the greatest gift that God can give.

Now that you have spent time with Jesus in the womb of the Blessed Virgin Mary, Jesus is calling you to 'remain', as He did with his disciples (John 15:4, 'remain in me'). He contrasts His heavenly glory, using the metaphor of the womb of his heavenly Father, with the suffering He endured from the moment of His incarnation and His suffering in the womb of His Mother. He endured this so that He could take away our sin and give us His own joys, destiny and eternal bliss. His deep sadness is that mankind repays Him with ingratitude. So, as with the first meditation, Jesus calls us to an attitude of gratitude. In a sense this is a call to stop the complaining and moaning which can be a part of our daily lives and give thanks to God for your life. He is revealing to you that ingratitude is the greatest sorrow for Him which shuts the door to him and leaves him outside in the cold. In contrast gratitude opens that door and welcomes him in. Ponder the blessings God has poured into your life and see any difficulties as crosses that God has or is using to sanctify you so that He can draw you to this great moment in your life when He can give you the greatest heavenly treasure. Offer Him gratitude that your exile in sadness and sorrow is ending, and heavenly bliss will soon be yours, even here on earth.

Eighth Excess of Love [of the Son of God]

"My child, don't abandon Me, but place your head upon the womb of My dear mother and you will hear, even from the outside, My moans and supplications. In seeing that neither My moans nor supplications of love move souls to offer Me any solace, I behave like the poorest of beggars who, stretching out his little hand, asks out of pity at least alms for [the good of] their [own] souls, for their affections and [the love in] their hearts. My love wants to win over the heart of man at any cost.

In seeing that after seven excesses of My love, man was still reluctant [in corresponding to My love] – he played deaf and neither cared for Me nor wished to give himself over to Me – My love excelled. My love should have ceased to pour itself out, but no, it wanted to overflow from its boundaries more abundantly. And so from the womb of My mother, My love extended My voice to every heart in the most insinuating of manners, with the most fervent prayers and with the most penetrating words. And do you know what I said to souls? 'My child, give Me your heart. I will give you everything you desire, so long as you give Me your heart in exchange. I have come down from heaven to seize this heart of yours. Oh please, do not deny Me this! Do not dash my hopes!'

In seeing man reluctant – to the point of many turning their back to Me – I then began to moan. Joining My little hands, and weeping with a voice stifled by sobs, I added: 'Oh! I am but a little beggar, and you do not wish to give Me your heart, not even as alms? Is this not a greater excess of My love – that the Creator, in His desire to approach man, should take the form of a little babe to avoid striking fear in him? That He should ask for man's heart at least as alms and, in seeing him refuse, implore, moan and weep?"

Then I heard Him say: "And do you not wish to offer Me your heart? Or perhaps you too want Me to moan, beg and cry for you to give Me your heart? Do you wish to deny Me the alms I ask?" And as He was saying this I heard Him as though sobbing. Whence I said: "O my Jesus, do not cry; I give you my heart and my entire being." Then, the interior voice continued: "Proceed further; continue onto the ninth excess of My love."

Jesus presents Himself in front of you as a poor beggar, wanting to win your heart. 'He became poor, that by his poverty you might become rich' (2 Cor. 8:9). Previously Jesus has asked us to listen to Him. Now He invites you; 'give me your heart'. He invites this of you so that he can enrich you, grant you peace, joy and love. Whatever you give Him, He can give you infinitely more. It is like a poor person giving a small coin to an extremely wealthy magnate, then that wealthy individual giving the poor person shares in his company, making him also extremely wealthy. The wealth is shared, poverty is removed. Luisa gave Jesus her heart and her entire being – can you? Ask Our Lady for the grace to give yourself to Jesus. Spend a moment receiving this grace and then move to the next excess.

Ninth Excess of Love [of the Son of God]

"My child, My state is increasingly sorrowful. If you love Me, keep your gaze fixed on Me to see if you can offer your Jesus some relief. A

little word of love, a caress or a kiss will console Me in My crying and in My afflictions.

My child, after I offered to man My eight excesses of love, and he requited them so badly, My love did not cease, but strove to add to the eighth a ninth excess. And this ninth excess are the yearnings, the sighs of fire and the flames of desire that caused Me to emerge from My mother's womb and embrace man. These [surgings of love] overwhelmed My little humanity, not yet born, to such an agonizing state that I reach the point of breathing My last. And as I was about to breathe My last, My divinity that is inseparable from My humanity, infused in Me small inhalations of life. And so I regained life to continue My agonizing state, and return again to the point of death.

Such is the ninth excess of My love: to agonize and to die of love continuously for souls. Oh, what a long agony of nine months! Oh, how love smothered Me and made Me die. Had I not possessed the divinity within My humanity, which infused life in Me every time I was about to die, love would have consumed Me before coming into this world."

Then He added: "Look at me, and listen closely: How I agonize, how My Heart throbs, pants and burns.

Look at me: In this moment I die..."

And He remained in deep silence.

I felt like dying; my blood froze in my veins and, trembling, I said to him: "My love and my life, do not die, do not leave me alone. You desire love; I will love You. I will not leave You ever again. Offer me your divine flames so that I may love You more, and be completely consumed for love of You."

In this final excess of love, you are invited to fix your gaze on Jesus:

'Fix your eyes on Jesus, the author and perfector of our faith.'

Hebrews 12:2

'We all, with unveiled face, gazing on the glory of the Lord, are being changed into his likeness from one degree of glory to another.'

2 Corinthians 3:18

This 'gazing' brings Jesus some relief. In reality, the relief was granted to Him when He was in the womb. This is because when Jesus was on earth in the flesh, everything he did had an eternal and infinite value. He knew you would be gazing on his face, bringing him relief, 2,000 years later. This is one of the beautiful mysteries of our faith. The gazing happens by the soul pondering deeply the Words of Christ, sitting in adoration, praying the rosary in a more contemplative fashion (rather than just repetition of the words), gazing on a statue or other image of Our Lord or His Blessed Mother. There are lots of ways that we can practice contemplation.

Another purpose of this 'gaze' is so that you can be released from your sin and experience a complete transformation. This brings Jesus consolation. How? Consider that Jesus suffered and died from the moment of His conception in the womb through to His last breath on the cross. Those sufferings were for the salvation of your soul, and to grant you the greatest of heaven's treasures, the Gift of Living in the Divine Will. The price paid for all of this were the sufferings of Jesus. Consequently, as the soul (you) corresponds to these graces that are being offered to you, and as you respond to the voice of the Lord Jesus, you are appropriating His sufferings in your life and bringing Him consolation.

Fiat!

2. The Gift of Living in the Divine Will

'Earnestly desire the higher gifts.'

1 Corinthians 12:31

I encourage the reader to ponder the words in this chapter carefully. In all of the years I have been teaching on this beautiful gift, this topic of 'what is this gift?' is the one that causes the most questions and confusion. So many people confuse 'living' in the Divine Will, with 'doing' the Divine Will. In His teachings to Luisa, Jesus makes it very clear that there is a huge distinction between the two. So, I encourage a deep meditation on this teaching, so that you are not confused but are deeply aware of this great grace that Jesus is presenting or infusing into your soul.

This gift is not a new devotion. It is not about 'doing' the Will of God. If it was, there would be nothing new to write about, because Saints have been writing on that very topic for nearly 2,000 years. This gift is about 'living' in the Divine Will. It is necessary for the person to already be 'doing' the Divine Will as something of a steppingstone. It is necessary for the soul to be living a life of virtue in order to be prepared to receive this great gift. Humility is absolutely necessary, because only the humble soul truly knows that everything she has in life comes from God and is well aware of her own nothingness compared to the fullness of God. The proud soul truly believes that everything she has comes by her own effort placing herself at the centre of everything she does and thinks. While the humble soul is exactly the opposite, loving God and regarding Him with all her heart, soul and mind. By being humble, we can receive this gift in its fullness, giving gratitude to the Father for our lives in this era.

Living in the Divine Will

What is the difference which exists between living in the Will of God and doing the Will of God? In order to understand what living in the Divine Will means, one has to dispose oneself to the greatest of sacrifices: that of not giving life, even in holy things, to one's own will. In the *Book of Heaven, Volume 17*, Luisa explains how she was worried about what she had written on the Divine Will. Jesus responds to her:

I was worried about what has been written on the living in the Divine Volition, and I was praying Jesus to give me more light in order to explain myself better, so that I might be able to clarify more this blessed living in the Divine Will to those to whom I am obliged to do so. And my sweet Jesus told me: 'My daughter, they do not want to understand. To live in my Will is to reign; to do my Will is to be submitted to my orders. The first state is to possess; the second is to receive my orders and execute them. To live in my Will is to make my Will one's own, as one's own thing, it is to dispose of It; to do my Will is to hold It as Will of God, not as one's own thing, nor can one dispose of It as one wants. To live in my Will is to live with one single Will – that of God; and since It is a Will all holy, all pure, all peace, and it is one single Will that reigns, there are no contrasts - everything is peace." [11]

In the last two thousand years since Jesus was on earth, and indeed, in the thousands of years prior to that from Adam to the Redemption, souls have strived to 'do' God's Will. However, they have done this striving in their own human will. The human will is one of the three faculties of the soul, the others being intellect and memory. By God's grace, the human will is strengthened so that it can break free from sin and live according to God's law, first revealed on Mount Sinai, but also revealed through the fullness of Sacred Scripture and the teachings of the Church. This is called 'doing' God's Will – obeying what He commands. It is also when the soul responds to the call to vocation, whether it is the call to marriage, the single life, or to religious life/priesthood. This is 'doing' God's Will. Responding to His call to serve Him.

In contrast to this, living in God's Will means that God fuses, or places, his own Will into the soul and enables the

---

[11] Piccarreta, Luisa, Book of Heaven, Volume 17, September 18th, 1924.

individual to have God's Will as the operative Will in their soul. Their own human will is subsequently going to be at rest, while the Divine Will is the Will that operates. For example, when I first started flowing in this gift in 2016, I had one meditation that I would use every day, 'Jesus, I give you my will in exchange for the gift of living in your Divine Will.' This is the entry point, as explained by Jesus to Luisa, and disposes the soul to cease using their own will as the operative will in the soul, and the Divine Will takes on that role. It puts your will to rest and enables God's Will to do all the work.

The wise soul will follow the simple guidance of the Lord Jesus as revealed to Luisa Piccarreta, which is the reason why I am doing this introductory book, and pray the simple prayers associated with the Divine Will throughout the day. The prayers I refer to are explained in this book and they serve to put the human will to rest and cause the Divine Will to be operative in the soul. As Jesus points out in the quote:

"*To live in my Will is to live with one single Will – that of God.*"

This simple action means that, as per the quote from Luisa, God's Divine Will becomes our own.

"To live in my Will is to make my Will one's own, as one's own thing." [12]

Initially this happens 'on loan' so to speak. The soul will inevitably go in and out of the Divine Will as it struggles with sin, and its own weaknesses. For example, many souls will say that they forget to do the various prayers associated with the Divine Will during the day, which means they are not attentive or faithful to the call of Christ to flow in the Divine Will all day, but rather they are focussing on their day-to-day cares and concerns. Also, if the soul falls into serious sin, the gift is immediately taken back by God because no sin can enter into His Divine Will. However, going to confession enables all to be restored.

Thus, the soul initially has the gift temporarily whilst it learns to completely abandon itself to God's Divine Will.

Referring again to what Jesus teaches Luisa – to live in the Divine Will means to reign, to possess, to have God's own Will as one's own possession. It means to have one single Will as the three Persons of the Trinity have just one Will between them. The soul shares that one Will which makes

---

[12] Piccarreta, Luisa, Book of Heaven, Volume 17, September 18th, 1924.

the soul all holy, all pure, all peace – because God's Will is all holy, all purity, all peace.

If you are thinking, 'can God give me his Will?' it is important to know that these teachings have been approved by multiple theologians who were appointed by the Vatican, and also by the Pontifical Gregorian University in Rome which approved a Doctoral Thesis on the Gift of Living in the Divine Will written by Fr Joseph Iannuzzi. Consequently, all that I am writing in this book that is rooted in the writings of Luisa Piccarreta, is drawn from Church approved writings. Any error will be either in the translation into English, or my poor explanations.

By a miracle of grace, the Divine Will of God can be infused into the soul which can have it as the operative Will for its own life. This was the original plan for the human soul, so it is a restoration of that which was lost by Adam 6,000 years ago when he sinned. The human will was originally meant to be a receptacle for the Divine Will. So for all of these thousands of years that people have been living according to their own will, with all of the chaos, confusion, wars, and sin that has caused, it has been because the human will not only disobeyed God, but was also empty of the Divine Will. Here we are, thousands of years later, and God can finally restore humanity to the great gift of having His own Will in operation in the human soul as it was meant to be. So rather than seeing this as something new, see it as a full restoration of what was originally intended when God formed Adam from the clay of the ground in the Garden of Eden. God is working a restoration project in millions of His children and all He needs from us is a 'fiat'. What is that 'fiat'? It is a simple expression of faith whereby we will say in prayer to God, 'let it be done to me' according to your word. In a chapter further on I will explain the importance of the 'fiat'.

Is this easy?

Human passions tremble before the Supreme Will, and would want to shun It; nor do they dare to even move, or oppose It, seeing that Heaven and earth tremble before this Holy Will. So, the first step of living in the Divine Will – what does it do? It lays the divine order in the depth of the soul, emptying her of what is human – of tendencies, of passions, of inclinations and the like. [13]

Note that Jesus declares that the person wants to shun the Divine Will. However, He also states that the passions do not want to oppose it because heaven and earth tremble before it. So there is a paradox. To shun, but to tremble, knowing you cannot oppose it. However, in His great mercy, Jesus provides us with a solution. When a person makes a decision to accept this heavenly treasure, the first thing that

[13] Piccarreta, L. Book of Heaven, Volume 17, September 18th 1924.

Jesus does is to 'lay the divine order in the depth of the soul'. This empties the soul of 'all that is human'. What belongs to this human order? 'Tendencies, passions, inclinations, and the like'. These tendencies that are troublesome are the tendencies towards sin. The pull towards immorality. As St Paul writes in Romans 7:19:

'For I do not do the good I want, but the evil I do not want is what I do.'

This is the battle that is rooted in the human will which saints have wrestled with for 2,000 years. I write that 'saints' have wrestled with this, because the average person won't wrestle with their tendency towards sin, they will merely immerse themselves in such a lifestyle as can be testified to by so many souls in the 20th and 21st centuries who have abandoned themselves to hedonistic lifestyles.

However, now we are at a turning point. God is offering us His own Divine Will to operate in our soul, governing us in a powerful way. Consequently, the first thing that happens when we give God our 'yes' or our 'fiat', is we become emptied of that which seeks to destroy us. Jesus reorders the human soul, emptying it, so as to prepare it to be filled to overflowing. So the soul can be reordered in God's way.

It is to be noted that the passions tremble before the Divine Will. Quite often, when the soul encounters God for the first time, great fear enters the soul. Not a craven fear, but a holy fear. This happened to the people of Israel when they encountered God at the foot of Mount Sinai:

'Now when all the people perceived the thunderings and the lightnings and the sound of the trumpet and the mountain smoking, the people were afraid and trembled; and they stood afar off.'

Exodus 20:18

This can often happen when the soul first encounters God, or God's representative (the Christian). The fear of God can descend into the soul and cause them to tremble before the Lord. This is healthy. The fear of God is the fear of offending Him, and when the soul has this 'trembling' encounter with God, they realise how much they have done in their life that has caused God offence.[14] For example, when St Peter encountered Jesus for the first time he exclaimed, 'Depart from me, for I am a sinful man, O Lord' (Luke 5:8).

---

[14] Please refer to the author's accompanying work, 'The Fear of the Lord' which teaches about this sanctifying gift of the Holy Spirit.

The response of the person is, as Jesus tells Luisa, 'to shun it.' So many will want to refuse this incredible gift before they finally accept the touch of Jesus on their soul. They will 'shun' it. What does this mean? Try this: persistently avoid, ignore, or reject (someone or something) through antipathy or caution. Are you one of those souls who has persistently ignored, rejected, or avoided this gift through either antipathy or caution? According to the words of Jesus, most people, if not all, will do exactly that. What is the solution? The key to overcome these stumbling blocks is to follow the counsel of St Luke at the start of his Gospel:

'I myself have carefully investigated everything from the beginning.'

Luke 1:3

Then continue reading this introductory book in which I am attempting to explain the basics of this gift so that you can begin to receive what Jesus is presenting to your soul. Careful investigation of the gifts that God is offering to our soul is helpful in fully receiving His graces. However, eventually one needs to yield to the grace by saying yes.

Give your fiat, say 'yes' to the gift.

To live with two wills

I invite you to deeply ponder these words of Jesus:

"On the other hand, to do my Will is to live with two wills, and when I give orders to do Mine, one feels the weight of one's own will, which causes contrasts. And even if one follows the orders of my Will with faithfulness, one feels the weight of one's rebellious nature, of one's passions and inclinations. How many Saints, though they may have reached the highest perfection, feel their own will waging war against them, keeping them oppressed; and many are forced to cry out: 'Who will free me from this body of death?'– that is, from this will of mine, which wants to give death to the good I want to do?" [15]

If we are just 'doing' the Will of God, then the human will is at work in the soul, whilst we are trying to live according to God's commands. This inevitably creates a conflict. The human will is inclined to evil and will want to freely give in to sin. Yet, it hears the call to live a different life, a more peaceful one, that will require much sacrifice, but will lead to peace. Is the soul willing to pass through this trial by fire in order to arrive at this place of peace, or will it prefer the short-term counterfeit 'peace' that comes through giving in to its passions? Jesus explains that when he gives the orders to do His Will, whether that be through a sermon, a book, a movie, a friend or spouse, the immediate reaction is to feel the weight of one's own will causing a contrast – a disagreement. Even following the Will of God (doing it), the

[15] Piccarreta, L. Book of Heaven, Volume 17, September 18th, 1924.

creature feels the weight of rebellion. The soul can be like the Israelite in the desert who though they responded to God's call and initially left the idols of Egypt in the past, they still wanted to build the golden calf in God's holy presence. This resembles the human will at war with the Divine Will.

"To live in my Will is to live as a son; to do my Will is to live as a servant. In the first state, what belongs to the father belongs to the son, and many times servants make more sacrifices than sons do; they have to expose themselves to more toilsome and more humble services, to cold, to heat, to traveling on foot. In fact, how much have my Saints not done in order to execute the orders of my Will? On the other hand, a son remains with his father, takes care of him, cheers him with his kisses and with his caresses; he commands the servants as if his father were commanding; if he goes out, he does not go on foot, but travels in a carriage. And while the son possesses everything that belongs to his father, servants are given only the retribution for the work they have done, remaining free to serve or not to serve their master; and if they do not serve, they have no more right to receive any further compensation. On the other hand, between father and son, no one can remove these rights: that the son possess the goods of the father; no law, either celestial or terrestrial, can remove these rights, nor unbind the sonship between father and son."[16]

[16] Piccarreta, L. Book of Heaven, Volume 17, September 18th, 1924.

One might think that one is living as a son, yet the Church is in agreement with Luisa. The first step in the process of canonisation is always 'Servant of God.' That is the state that we have found ourselves for thousands of years. Now we live in this wonderful new era in which Jesus wants to transform us interiorly in a very different way so that we truly become sons and daughters of the Living God. He wants to give us His own Will to reign in us, so that we are no longer servants, but sons. He wants what belongs to the Father (His Will) to belong to us.

'No longer do I call you servants, for the servant does not know what his master is doing; but I have called you friends, for all that I have heard from my Father I have made known to you.'

John 15:15

So, we are still 'doing' His Will, but we are now given more, we are actually given His own Will so that we can possess all of the goods that belong to the Father.

Heaven on Earth

"My daughter, the living in my Will is the living that is closest to the blessed of Heaven;"'

Up to the time of Luisa the highest height of holiness that was attainable on earth was that of mystical marriage, spiritual marriage. From the time of Luisa receiving this greatest of all gifts, God has given us an remarkable new grace. The soul that has possession of the Divine Will, who fully lives in it, can now be in the same state as the Blessed in Heaven. Multiple mystics of the 20th century experienced this unique grace, which can be found in their writings, like St Faustina who had it revealed to her that her soul was in the same state as the Blessed in Heaven. There are others, like the Canadian mystic Dina Belanger.

This state is not something that the soul attains to or merits. It is a grace that God gives to the soul, and one aspect of the definition of grace is 'unmerited favour'. "Grace is favour, the free and undeserved help that God gives us to respond to his call to become children of God".[17] The first step is to accept the lower graces that God grants to the soul, like the simplest 'fiat' that Jesus is inviting you to make so that He can fuse his Will into your soul. If you accept this gift, then the state of beatitude on earth will be within your grasp. You can receive the bright, blazing light of God's glory shining in your soul in all of its brilliance, rather than the dim light of a flickering candle.

The Gift

This is another explanation of the gift by Jesus, as recorded by Luisa in her diaries on the Divine Will:

---

[17] CCC, Article 1996.

"Living in the Divine Will is so distant from one who does my Will and is faithfully submitted to my orders, just as Heaven is distant from the earth, just as the distance between a son and a servant, and between a king and a subject. And besides, this is a gift which I want to give in these times, so sad - that they may not only do my Will, but possess It. Am I perhaps not free to give whatever I want, whenever I want, and to whomever I want? Is a master not free to say to his servant: 'Live in my house, eat, take, command like another me'? And so that no one may prevent him from possessing his goods, he legitimizes this servant as his own son, and gives him the right to possess. If a rich man can do so, much more can I do it." [18]

These words from Jesus clearly reveal that this is a gift, not something that we can attain by good works, by coercive behaviour, by self-righteousness. It is a gift that God is giving to the Church in this era of Sanctification. It is also the greatest gift that God could ever give. In His own words:

"This living in my Will is the greatest gift I want to give to creatures. My goodness wants to make ever greater display of love toward creatures; and since I have given them everything, and have nothing else

---

[18] Piccarreta, L. Book of Heaven, Volume 17, September 18th, 1924.

to give to make Myself loved, I want to give them the gift of my Will, so that, by possessing It, they may love the great good they possess."[19]

However, Jesus issues Luisa with a caution, that of not understanding. Coming into the light has always involved suffering, that of being in the bright light of God's divine revelation. Consequently, even when He was on earth, Jesus had to speak in many parables so that the hearers would spend time contemplating the mysteries He was revealing. That process of deeply meditating upon the mysteries involved a gradual walking out of intellectual darkness into the bright light of God's revealed truth. To facilitate this process we need to dispose our hearts towards receiving this greatest of all gifts:

"And do not be surprised if you see that they do not understand. In order to understand, they would have to dispose themselves to the greatest of sacrifices: that of not giving life, even in holy things, to their own will. Then would they feel the possession of Mine, and would touch with their own hands what it means to live in my Will. You, however, be attentive, and do not be bothered by the difficulties they raise; and I, little by little, will make my way to make them understand the living in my Will."[20]

---

[19] Piccarreta, L. Book of Heaven, Volume 17, September 18th, 1924.

[20] Piccarreta, L. Book of Heaven, Volume 17, September 18th, 1924.

Consequently, the work is done 'little by little.' This is God's patient way of working with the rather stubborn human creature, who simply does not want to accept God's divine revelation. This is partly because we have a tendency to want to do things our own way (the sin of pride), rather than rely on what God is revealing to us; in this case through the writings of Luisa Piccarreta. However, those who can humble themselves and give way to the work of the Divine Master, will find it easier to accept this beautiful gift, receive it, grow in it, and eventually take possession of it. This results in the greatest of all happiness, peace, joy and love.

To summarise

The gift of living in the Divine Will:

- **Is primarily to give God the perfect return of glory on behalf of all human creatures that He was due to receive from the beginning.**
- **Is the free gift of God, given to those who wish to receive it**
- **Is where the soul has the Divine Will, God's own Will, as the operative Will in the soul**
- **Is for the soul who is faithful and attentive, paying careful attention to the words of Christ regarding this gift, as revealed to the Italian mystic, Luisa Piccarreta**

- **Is a participation in God's one eternal act.**
- **Is a grace raising the soul to the eternal mode of prayer and action. Please note this point especially as this term is used in subsequent chapters.**

Fiat!

3. The First Step in the Divine Will

Come Divine Will, read in my reading.

'For the fountain of life is with You;
In Your light we see light.'
Psalm 36:9

We have now read the prelude and disposed our hearts to the teaching of Jesus, which is a very bright light in the soul. Hopefully our desire for this gift is increasing as well, that is a necessary disposition in order for the soul to receive the graces associated with this gift. In the previous chapter we saw what exactly this beautiful gift is; a participation in the **eternal mode of prayer and action**, participation in **God's one eternal act**. Now, we look at the first step we need to take in order to enter the Divine Will of God, resignation.

The first step to enter the Will of God is resignation. The soul who is resigned to the Divine Will comes to make of God her favourite food.[21]

Let us take that first step together right now. All we need do is quietly speak, or even think, *Jesus, I resign myself to your*

[21] Piccarreta, L., Book of Heaven, Volume 6, November 8th, 1905.

Divine Will. Amen.' The first step truly is that simple. The actual process of being completely resigned to the Divine Will might require more grace on God's behalf, and more desire on behalf of the soul (you) but taking that first simple step is most important.

Luisa writes:

After I struggled very much, He came for just a little and told me: "My daughter, it happens to the soul who resigns herself to my Will as to someone who, drawing near a beautiful food in order to see it, feels the desire to eat it, and as his desire is excited, he begins to enjoy that food, and to transmute it into his flesh and into his blood. Had he not seen that beautiful food, the desire could not have come, he could not have experienced its taste, and would have continued to remain on an empty stomach." [22]

Note that Luisa begins the entry, 'after I struggled very much'. Much like a baby bird climbing out of an egg, or a child coming to birth. Whereas they have a physical struggle, we all have our struggles in the spiritual life. We all struggle in bringing something new to birth in our lives, whether that is physical, emotional, or spiritual. Indeed, the spiritual birth pangs can be incredibly painful because they can last for a long time and there is no pain relief. Therefore, do not be afraid of the spiritual birth pangs, they are going to lead to

[22] Piccarreta, L., Book of Heaven, Volume 6, November 8th, 1905.

blessings that will cause the birth pains to be a distant memory.

Jesus makes reference to the act of giving birth when He speaks of the sorrow His disciples will have because of His death and resurrection. However, could He also be referring to our sorrow due to the sufferings of this life before we are born into heaven?

'When a woman is in labour, she has pain, because her hour has come; but when she is delivered of the child, she no longer remembers the anguish, for joy that a child is born into the world. So you have sorrow now, but I will see you again and your hearts will rejoice, and no one will take your joy from you.'

John 16:21, 22

St Paul wrote to the Church in Galatia which had strayed back into the flesh and were performing circumcision on new believers. He chastises them for this behaviour, and then declares:

'My little children, with whom I am again in travail until Christ be formed in you.'

Galatians 4:19

Jesus calls the first motion of resignation as being like a hungry soul seeing beautiful food, and thus having both the appetite and the desire for the food. This is describing a spiritual reality with physical metaphors. Your soul is hungry and thirsty. The only food for the soul is God:

'My food is to do the Will of Him who sent me, and to accomplish His work.'

John 4:34

'God alone is enough.'

St Teresa of Avila

The Word of God feeds the soul; the Eucharist feeds the soul on the Body, Blood, Soul, and Divinity of Christ; prayer fills the soul with the Holy Spirit, especially contemplative prayer which when authentic, enables the soul to be possessed by the Spirit. God is the only life of the soul.

'Open wide your mouth and I will fill it.'

Psalm 80:10

Just as feeding the body brings the desires and appetites back within manageable boundaries, bringing contentment and peace to the body, so does God bring the soul back from anxieties, fears, worries, and sin into the boundaries of His creation in which is peace, love, joy, hope, faithfulness, etc. This journey begins with the soul resigning itself to the Divine Will.

'Now, such is resignation for the soul. As she resigns herself, in her very resigning she sees a divine light, and this light dispels what prevents her from seeing God; and as she sees God, she desires to enjoy Him; and while she enjoys Him, she feels as if she were eating Him, in such a way as to feel God Himself all transmuted into herself.' [23]

It is important to recognise that the soul 'seeing' the divine light, is not like the physical eyes seeing the sun. Indeed, spiritual experiences, such as the soul seeing a divine light, are very different from physical experiences. For example, if your eyes were shut, you could probably notice (see, discern) when the sun comes out from behind a cloud because you could feel the heat of it on your body (presuming a warm summer's day). So, although you can't 'see', you can 'see' but using a different sense. Instead of using eyesight, you are using the feeling of warmth on the body.

Translate that into spiritual language. How does the soul know it sees God? First, to recognise that the soul is blind in its interiority. It cannot see God. It cannot see the spiritual journey it needs to take in order to arrive in His presence.

---

[23] Piccarreta, L., Book of Heaven, Volume 6, November 8th, 1905.

In the *Dark Night of the Soul* by St John of the Cross, he tells us that the soul is blinded from seeing God by the delights of the senses. In Luisa's writings, Jesus tells us that this blindness is removed by an act of resignation to the Divine Will. That act opens up the eyes of the soul to God, and several things happen for us to know we are seeing God spiritually. For example, there is a stronger desire to encounter God in prayer even if there are no 'consolations' (nice experiences) in prayer, the desire is still there. The soul is 'hungry and thirsty' for God. Another sign of the soul 'seeing' God is the soul gains a very strong awareness of its own weaknesses, sin, failure, shortcomings. It discovers a stronger dependence on God (which is the virtue of humility growing). The seeing of the sin is a sign of the bright light of God's presence in the soul. Also, the soul notices that the things of this world are transient, fading, rubbish, passing away:

'Indeed I count everything as loss because of the surpassing worth of knowing Christ Jesus my Lord. For his sake I have suffered the loss of all things, and count them as refuse, in order that I may gain Christ'

Philippians 3:8

A consequence of this encounter with God is that the soul attaches less importance to the material things of this world. The soul is captivated by God. Even if it doesn't physically see him, the contemplation of the divinity captures the soul. That contemplation is generally carried out in 'darkness' to the senses, but the soul is in light. The fruit of this is peace, joy, love, hope, faith – all the virtues flourishing.

'Therefore, it follows that the first step is to resign oneself; the second is to desire to do the Will of God in everything; the third is to make of It one's favourite food, daily; the fourth is to consume the Will of God within one's own. But if one does not take the first step, he will remain empty of God.' [24]

Therefore, you can 'see' that God has called you to take that first step of resignation, which will cure any spiritual blindness you might have, and leave you hungry and thirsty for God alone.

This resignation needs to be coupled with the grace of self-knowledge, (explained a little further on). Jesus talks to Luisa about the grace of self-knowledge:

The knowledge of self empties the soul of herself and fills her with God. [25]

---

[24] Piccarreta, L., Book of Heaven, Volume 6, November 8th, 1905.
[25] Piccarreta, L., Book of Heaven, Volume 6, October 12th, 1905.

Note that the above entry on resignation concludes that the soul will remain empty if she does not take that first step of resigning herself, and that the entry on self-knowledge begins by describing how the soul can be filled with God. However, the purpose of this book is not to spend a great deal of time analysing what it means to be filled with God, it is to introduce the reader to the concept. A further study on 'filled with God' will be forthcoming.

Whereas the Gift of Living in the Divine Will is a new grace offered to the Church in this era in which we live, the knowledge of self is not new. It is a grace of the contemplative life, given to those who wish to proceed into the depths of God, and to leave behind the vanities of this life. It is a treasure, a wonderful grace that helps to sanctify the soul. One cannot move forward in the spiritual life, to become a serious contemplative, and thus eventually a saint, if one does not have a healthy self-knowledge. It is worth noting that Jesus talks about self-knowledge a mere four weeks before he tells the soul about the first step in the Divine Will. There is a beautiful order to his teaching:

The prelude – what is the gift? - self-knowledge - the first step of resignation.

Of course, he also teaches Luisa about the virtues, suffering, humility, grace, and a plenitude of other topics pertaining to the spiritual life. I am merely focussing on the above four at the moment. My focus on self-knowledge is partly the fruit of having many discussions with people over the years and seeing them truly not grasp the importance of it, nor of living the grace out in their daily lives.

On the topic of self-knowledge Luisa writes:

Continuing in my usual state, blessed Jesus came for just a little and told me: "My daughter, the knowledge of self empties the soul of herself and fills her with God. Not only this, but in the soul there are many receptacles, and everything that can be seen in the world takes its place in these receptacles - something more, something less, according to the concept of them that she makes for herself." [26]

What are these receptacles? This is from an Italian lady who grew up near Corato, the village where Luisa lived: "In my parents' apartment upstairs the receptacle, which in Italian is 'ripostiglio,' is the smallest room in the house, although quite big. We would call it a utility room. There is a wall of shelves. We keep shoes, ladder, brooms and hoover, but also food reserves and so on. When filled with 'good' useful things it is a functional room where one reposes goods.

Jesus says we should repose good things and not fill it with rubbish, which sometimes can happen, like empty boxes, or whatever we have that is not essential. In the little apartment

---

[26] Piccarreta, L., Book of Heaven, Volume 6, October 12th, 1905.

downstairs the ripostiglio is one square metre or an area hidden by a curtain. Inside there is also a cupboard with medical supplies and so on and the useful items needed to clean. Perhaps we can ponder on these last things kept in it. If we apply this thinking to the soul, the receptacle will be an interior part of the soul where we have attachments to things that we don't use, or rarely use. You might have a book on a shelf that you read once, but hasn't been read in years, and you probably won't ever read again. Or some clothes hanging up that you wore a few years ago, which are kept 'just in case,' but you know you won't wear them again. It could be the tools in the garage, the DVD's, etc. Items that you have retained because you *want* them there, but you know you won't use or need them. These are physical items, that have found a place in your 'receptacle'.

'Now, the soul who knows herself and is filled with God, knowing that she is 'a nothing', or rather, a fragile, rotten and stinking vase, is well wary of letting more filthy rot enter into her interior, which is the things that can be seen in the world.'[27]

The things that can be seen in the world – like the objects previously mentioned – which are seen and are now in your soul. You are attached to them, but you were created for God alone.

[27] Piccarreta, L., Book of Heaven, Volume 6, October 12th, 1905.

'One who had a rotten wound and kept gathering more rot to put it on his wound, would be quite crazy. Now, the knowledge of self brings with it the knowledge of the things of the world, and therefore how everything is vanity, fleetingness, goods that are only masked, deceits, inconstancy of creature. So, knowing how things are in themselves, she is well wary of letting them enter into herself, and so all those receptacles remain filled with the virtues of God.' [28]

This self-knowledge is a good honesty checker. For example, you might say 'oh, that old thing. I am not attached to that, but I do like having it around.' Under the microscope of authentic self-knowledge, you have an unhealthy attachment to whatever *that* is and it prevents your growth in the spiritual life. The first step to freedom is recognising the attachment and allowing God's purifying touch to free you. Being released from your bondage to it, and having the receptacle that it can being filled with God's virtues instead. For example, instead of the receptacle having the old shirt in it, it could be filled with God's eternal peace instead. An exchange worth considering.

Step one in your journey in the Divine Will – 'Jesus, I resign myself to your Divine Fiat'

Fiat!

---

[28] Piccarreta, L., Book of Heaven, Volume 6, October 12th, 1905.

4. Entering in

'You gave them bread from heaven for their hunger and brought forth water for them from the rock for their thirst, and you told them to go in to possess the land which you had sworn to give them.'

Nehemiah 9:15

It is all about what God wants to give to His creatures, and what we are willing to receive from His providential goodness. In the above scripture we could read it that the bread is the Eucharist, the water is the Holy Spirit, and the land that God wants us to take possession of is the Kingdom of the Divine Will.

'Do not be afraid little flock, for your Father has chosen to give you the Kingdom.'

Luke 12:32

We can also find Jesus explicitly stating that He wants us to take possession of the Kingdom of the Divine Will:

"There is nothing I did that did not have as its primary purpose man's taking possession of My Will, and I of his. This was my primary purpose in Creation, and this was also the very purpose of My Redemption. The sacraments I instituted and the many graces imparted to my saints have been seeds, means to let man attain to the possession of My Will." [29]

We should carefully note that this gift which is being offered to us by the Lord Jesus was the primary purpose of Creation and Redemption. We might look at the crucifixion that Jesus underwent and think it is all about salvation. However, Jesus reveals to Luisa that the primary purpose of His sufferings, death, Resurrection and Ascension, was to reestablish humanity in the Kingdom of the Divine Will for the glory of the Father. It is so that the Divine Will can reign in the human soul, and that the human will can be at rest. This enables God to receive a perfect return of glory from all human creatures.

It may sound easy, that all we need to do is to desire and receive the gift on offer. Whilst it is true that all we need to do is desire and receive the gift, there are conditions that require us to be appropriately disposed to receiving this incredible gift from God. Here is the entry point:

---

[29] Piccarreta, L. Book of Heaven, Volume 14, September 11th, 1922.

'My daughter, to enter into My Will, the soul does nothing other than remove the pebble of her will. Because the little pebble of her will prevents her, just like water is prevented from flowing from the shore to run elsewhere because the pebble impedes the flow. But if the soul removes the pebble of her will, in that same instant she flows in Me, and I in the soul. She finds all of My treasures at her disposal: light, strength, assistance and all that she desires. That is why there are no ways, no doors, no keys; It is enough that the soul desires it, and everything is done.' [30]

This is simple and requires you to pray to Jesus, 'Lord, I give you the little pebble of my will, in exchange for the gift of living in Your Divine Will.' The whole giving and receiving rests on the soul desiring this gift. This desiring is nothing new. Everything you have in your life has probably been the fruit of what you have desired. On a purely material basis, that can often be clearly seen. If you apply the same thinking to your spiritual life, that which you desire, you will obtain.

'Delight yourself in the LORD;
And He will give you the desires of your heart.'
Psalm 37:4

[30] Piccarreta, L. Book of Heaven, Volume 12, February 16th, 1921.

We can read this as 'if you delight in God He will give you all of the pleasures of this world,' but if we desired all of the pleasures of this world we would not be delighting in the Lord. If we read this in the context of the primary purpose of Creation and Redemption, then we delight the Lord by desiring above all things, the Kingdom of the Divine Will. If we desire it, Jesus will give it to us. It will flow in us and we will flow in it.

On the other hand, the one thing that impedes the Divine Will from flowing in us is our own will. This human will of ours leaves us weak, in darkness, isolated from God, and outside of the Kingdom of God's Divine Will. The human will cannot have life in that beautiful kingdom because it has a tendency to oppose it. Also, the human will is too constricted to receive that Kingdom. It is too inclined to self and sin. None of this can enter into the Divine Will. Thus, in order to delight in God the human will must be put to rest, which is accomplished by the grace of God. The Divine Will must be constantly given freedom to reign, again by the grace of God.

Many souls often feel unworthy of these great graces that God is offering to them. This is nothing new, and Sacred Scripture testifies to several arguments that holy souls of the past had with God when He offered them unique graces. Moses argued with God and asked Him to send Aaron;

Jeremiah said he was too young; Isaiah said he was sinful; Peter told Jesus to leave him alone because he was a sinful man. One of the few souls who fully received all God wanted to entrust to her was a young lady called Mary who merely enquired as to how God's plan would come about. She then gave her wholehearted 'fiat'.

However, it is to be noted that Jesus often chooses the weak:

"The greater the work I want to do, the more I choose abject, poor, ignorant souls, with no outward appearance which may expose them. The abject state of the soul will serve as safe custody for my work. The thieves of self-esteem and love of self will not pay attention to her, knowing her inability. And she, humble and trembling, will carry out the office entrusted by Me, knowing that she has done nothing by herself, but that I did everything in her." [31]

Consequently, if you are a poor, ignorant soul (which we all are) then you are in very good company and without excuse. Also, please note the last line in the above quote, the golden rule… 'she has done nothing by herself, but … I did everything in her.' This is the golden rule. The work is that of the Lord Jesus. Our task is to give Jesus a constant 'fiat'

[3131] Piccarreta, L., Book of Heaven, Volume 12, January 17th, 1921.

(let it be done) and His work is to establish His kingdom in our midst.

Our task is to take possession of Jesus's acts especially those of His hidden life – allowing Jesus to do His work in us and with us:

"By lowering Myself to all those little actions and those acts which men exercise during their daily life, such as eating, sleeping, drinking, working, starting the fire, sweeping, etc. - all acts which no one can do without - I made flow inside their souls a tiny divine coin of incalculable price. Therefore, if my Passion redeemed them, my hidden Life provided each human action, even the most insignificant one, with Divine merit and with infinite value."[32]

It is His work, we can do nothing without His aid:

'Apart from me you can do nothing'

John 15:5

Again, it is very hard for us to grasp this statement. It requires healthy self-knowledge because human pride has left us believing quite firmly that we can do so much without God's help. Indeed, how many call on God only in a

---

[32] Piccarreta, L., Book of Heaven, Volume 11, August 14th, 1912.

moment of desperation, suggesting that God was not present during the rest of their life. Actually, God is ever present. He feeds us, clothes us, enables us to breathe, keeps the heart beating, the blood flowing, the intellect thinking, the memory remembering:

'He (The Holy Spirit) will teach you all things, and remind you of all that I said to you.'

Jn 14:26

We are completely dependent on God for everything that pertains to life and living. One of the graces of Luisa's writings is learning how much God is involved in every aspect of our lives. Rather than being the one we seek in an emergency when things have become desperate, instead He is constantly present: supplying, helping, supporting, guiding, keeping an eye, etc. He keeps every atom of our being in existence at every moment of the day.

This is our God.

So what is our role in this? Pretty much the same task as we have always had; to hear God's Word and respond accordingly:

'Keep all the commandments that you may be strong…and take possession.'

Deuteronomy 11:8

The only food for our soul is God. Keeping His commandments, His Word makes us strong, increases the strength of our soul, in order that we can take possession of this Kingdom that He is offering us. This involves deeply meditating on every word that He speaks to us, whether from the Word of God (Bible), or from the writings of Saints, including Servants of God like Luisa. By reading and rereading the Book of Heaven, the soul grows in strength and can fervently live the life that God always intended us to live. This will enable us to take possession, as God Wills that we do, and become the children that He desires we become.

Just keep his Word, let it become your food, and you will take possession.

Fiat!

5. Fusing in the Divine Will

Come Divine Will, read in my reading.

'He measured a thousand, and it was a river I could not pass through, for the water had risen; it was deep enough to swim in, a river that could not be passed through.'

Ezekiel 47:5

Luisa invites the child of the Divine Will to invoke it in everything they do, hence the opening to the chapter 'come Divine Will…' This is also part of the process of fusing yourself into the Divine Will with every act that we do. Hence:

'May your life on earth be completely fused in me. Do not do any act without making it (first) enter within me.'[33]

For many centuries the Church has taught the Faithful that God's life is 'infused' into the soul by the action of grace. For example, in the Catechism section on the theological virtues it states: 'They are infused by God into the souls of

[33] Piccarreta, L., Book of Heaven volume 12, March 18th, 1917.

the faithful to make them capable of acting as His children and of meriting eternal life.'[34]

In the writings of Luisa, the soul is invited to make a profound reciprocal movement, to fuse herself into the Divine Will. This is a unique invitation and grace from God. It was not a form of prayer available to the Faithful in previous eras but is unique to this era in the life of the Church.

Jesus speaks of the importance of fusing oneself in the Divine Will as Luisa begins by fusing herself in the Divine Will:

I started to fuse my entire poor being in the Supreme Will, and as I was doing so, I noticed the heavens opening, and I went up to meet the whole heavenly court, and all of heaven came towards me. And my sweet Jesus said to me: "My daughter, fusing yourself in My Will is the most solemn act, the greatest one, the most important of your entire life. To fuse yourself in My Will is to enter the eternal mode, to embrace it, to impress upon it a (mystical) kiss and to receive the treasury of the blessings that My Eternal Will contains. What is more, as the soul fuses herself in Our Supreme Will, all (heaven) goes out to meet this soul to convey to it all the blessings and glory that they possess. The angels, the saints and the Divinity itself convey everything to this soul, knowing that what they convey is conveyed in God's Will where everything is safe. What is more, in receiving these blessings, the soul

[34] Catechism of the Catholic Church, Article 1813

multiplies them through its acts in the Divine Will and, in return, gives to all of heaven double honour and glory." [35]

To Luisa, Jesus reveals what happens when she fuses herself in the Divine Will, similar to how God reveals to other souls what happens when a soul prays, does penance, receives communion or goes to confession. Although you and I might not have this privilege of seeing the result of our act of fusing ourselves, Luisa conveys it to us through her writing. Thus, one act of fusing ourselves in the Divine Will ('Jesus,I fuse myself into your Divine Will') causes the above to take place. All of heaven comes toward us, heaven and earth are put in motion.

Jesus also reveals to Luisa the importance of each act of fusing oneself. Note the distinction between what is important to God, and that which is important to us on earth. For example, if one goes without any nourishment for a 24-hour period, the appetite can quickly dominate one's life. Eating and drinking might become the top priority, the most important thing, the life-saving necessity. If a person doesn't eat for just one day, missing out on a few meals, then the appetites can quickly dominate a person's behaviours, way of thinking, desires. They will rapidly begin craving food, drink, a meal. These become the total focus of the person to the extent that a person might well exchange

---

[35] Piccarreta, L., Book of Heaven, volume 17, January 4th, 1925.

anything they have in life for some food. Some would even sacrifice their personal dignity.

On the other hand, if one is not missing anything of life's basic human necessities, then the priorities change and it might become important to have a nice bottle of wine for a meal, or to have a certain make of car to drive; alternatively, to have a certain property in which to live, in a certain part of the city or country. These become the important acts of our life.

Jesus shows us God's perspective:

'Fusing yourself in My Will is the most solemn act, the greatest one, the most important of your entire life.' [36]

From God's perspective, fusing oneself in the Divine Will is the most important act of a person's life. So, our bodily necessities play a secondary role when it comes to God's viewpoint. Hence the words of Christ:

'Seek first the Kingdom of God… and all these things will be added to you.'

Matthew 6:33

---

[36] Piccarreta, L., Book of Heaven, Volume 12, March 18th, 1917.

The soul that fuses herself to the Divine Will repeats what Jesus did and still does in Heaven, doing in Him what He does Himself, therefore praying, repairing, satisfying appeasing, like a sentry of honour before the Divine Throne acquiring glory. When fusing and losing herself in the Divine Will, the soul, doing everything Jesus does, attracts the fruitful word of life from Jesus. The "I love you" that fills heaven and earth, circulates in the Saints, descends in the hearts of creatures in need, penetrates Purgatory and invests the elements of new life.[37]

The beauty is that in order to fuse oneself in the Divine Will, one can just do it. The soul needs to be in a state of grace, which is true for anything concerning a meaningful relationship with God, and then they can fuse every act of their day into the Divine Will, whether that act is emotional (love), spiritual (prayer), physical (eating), or psychological (thinking, including mental prayer). All of these different things are the various acts.

"My daughter how beautiful it is to see a soul fuse itself in My Will! As it fuses itself in It, the created heartbeat takes its place and Life in the Uncreated Heartbeat to form a single beat. And they flow and beat together with the Eternal Palpitation. This is the greatest happiness of the human heart to beat in the Eternal Heartbeat of its Creator. My

---

[37] Piccarreta, L., Book of Heaven, Volume 12, March 28th, 1917.

Volition puts it into flight, and the human palpitation is hurled into the Centre of its Creator". [38]

We can fuse our heartbeat, breathing, and the flow of our blood into the Divine Will, as was God's original order in the human body. The Father to beat in our heartbeat and fill our will: the Son to flow in our blood and fill our intellect: the Spirit to breathe in our breathing and fill our memories. The important thing is the conscious decision to fuse every act into the Divine Will at the start of the day, during the day, and at the end of the day.

What does fusing do?

"My daughter, when a soul fuses herself in my Will, it happens as when two containers, full of different fluids, are poured one into the other: the first remains filled with what the second contained, and the second with the content of the first. In the same way, the creature remains filled with Me, and I with her. And since my Will contains sanctity, beauty, power, love, etc., by filling herself with Me, fusing and abandoning herself in my Will, the soul comes to be filled with my sanctity, with my love, with my beauty, etc., in the most perfect way given to a creature. And I feel I am filled with her, and finding in her my sanctity, my beauty, my love, etc. I look at these things as if they were her own, and I like her so much as to become enamoured, in such a way as to keep her jealously in my inmost Heart, enriching her and

---

[38] Piccarreta, L., Book of Heaven, Volume 17, October 6th, 1924.

embellishing her continuously with my divine qualities, to be ever more delighted and enamoured." [39]

Fusing ourselves into the Divine Will enables the soul to enter the eternal mode of prayer and action. It means that everything the soul does is operating in God's eternal mode of operation.[40] It elevates the soul. It also enables the soul to receive the treasury of everything that the Divine Will contains.

For the majority, if not for all of us, this act of fusing in the Divine Will might well come without the encounter that Jesus revealed to Luisa. That is because of the nature of grace:

'Since it belongs to the supernatural order, grace escapes our experience and cannot be known except by faith. We cannot therefore rely on our feelings or our works to conclude that we are justified and saved.' [41]

Bearing in mind that grace escapes our experience and we cannot rely on our feelings, it is likely that when you or I fuse ourselves into the Divine Will, as you might wish to do

---

[39] Piccarreta, L., Book of Heaven, Volume 11, August 27th 1915.

[40] See chapter on 'The Gift of Living in the Divine Will for a further explanation of this phrase.

[41] Catechism of the Catholic Church, Article 2005.

right now (Lord Jesus, I fuse myself into your Will, come Divine Will, read in my reading), there is no blinding light, no coming forth of thousands of angels to be seen; heaven is not eclipsing your midday sun, or causing a blazing light to shine at night, (depending on when you are reading this). However, Luisa reveals that this is precisely what happens. Grace is beyond our experience.

The angels and saints convey everything to the soul that fuses herself into God's Divine Will. Thus, you do one act of fusing yourself, and it invokes the intercession of many angels and saints, bringing to your soul all that is needed for your growth in the Divine Will. This growth in His Will is the most important part of our lives, so you can be assured that this is what heaven wills for you. Although it might not always be what you 'want', it is definitely what every human being 'needs'.

What follows is perhaps the most important point of all the acts in the Divine Will, the act of fusing oneself in the Divine Will gives 'to all of heaven double honour and glory.' We must remind ourselves regularly that the purpose of our existence is to glorify God, and by following the teaching of Jesus in the diaries of Luisa, we can more perfectly glorify God. By fusing oneself in the Divine Will, that very simple act, we give heaven double honour and glory.

In addition to this:

"The soul who fuses itself in My Will receives, as though in deposit, all of My divine and eternal treasures. The very saints compete with each other in order to deposit their merits in the soul fused in My Will, because they feel in this soul the glory and the power of My Will, and they feel glorified in a divine way by the lowliness of this soul." [42]

Consequently, when you fuse yourself, so simply and beautifully, in the Divine Will, with your simple acts, Jesus can deposit all of His divine and eternal treasures in your soul. These treasures might not seem overly important to a soul that is trying to make her way in this material world in which the treasures of the spiritual life are veiled and hidden. However, if we just examine a couple of treasures that Jesus can deposit in your soul it might reveal something new for you. For example, the world makes war incessantly. People fight people, nations fight nations. Yet, for the Kingdom of the Divine Will, peace is the constant. Possessing the Divine Will, possessing the Kingdom of the Divine Will, is possessing peace. That peace of soul is beyond anything one can describe on earth because it is an interior state. It is not exterior yet, but it will have an impact on the exterior world in which we live. It is not from this world, it is from God. Consequently, it is not possible to describe in worldly terms:

---

[42] Piccarreta, L., Book of Heaven, Volume 17, January 4th, 1925.

'And the peace of God, which surpasses all comprehension, will guard your hearts and minds in Christ Jesus.'

Phl. 4:7

The Greek word used for 'comprehension' in this passage is 'nous.' It can also be used to describe intellect, understanding, thinking. That peace is beyond our understanding, intellectual ability, our thinking. It is a union of the soul with God, and the soul simply cannot grasp God. He who is infinite, uniting Himself with the finite soul, bringing her His own peace. This is one of the treasures of God's Kingdom that Christ wishes to visit your soul with, and with an abundance of it. Jesus is not a measured giver. He always gives without measuring the gift.

'He gives the Spirit without measure.'

John 3:34

This is just one of the treasures, there are infinitely more, and all you need do is live each day fusing every act in His Divine Will.

Fiat!

6. Acts in the Divine Will

'I am confident of this, that he who began a good work in you will complete it until the day of Christ Jesus.'

Philippians 1:6

Each act that we do in the Divine Will enables us to grow in it.

Continuing in my usual state, my always lovable Jesus, on coming, told me: "My daughter, each time the soul does her acts in my Will, she grows more and more before Me in wisdom, in goodness, power and beauty. In fact, as she keeps repeating her acts in my Will, she takes as many bites of wisdom, of goodness, etc.; and the soul grows from that food with which she feeds herself. This is why in the Holy Gospel it is written of Me that I grew in wisdom before God and before men. As God, I could neither grow nor decrease; my growth was no other than my Humanity which, growing in age, came to multiply my acts in the Supreme Volition; and each additional act that I did was additional growth in the wisdom of my Celestial Father. And this growth of mine was so true, that even creatures noticed it. Each one of my acts ran in the immense sea of the Divine Will; and as I operated, I nourished Myself with this celestial food. It would take too long to tell you of the seas of wisdom, of goodness, of beauty, of power, that my Humanity swallowed in each additional act It did. The same happens to the soul.

My daughter, the sanctity in my Will grows at each instant - there is nothing that can escape growing, and that the soul cannot let flow in the infinite sea of my Will. The most indifferent things - sleep, food, work, etc. - can enter into my Will and take their place of honour in It as agents of my Will."[43]

Prior to Jesus giving us this beautiful gift, the way to grow in sanctity was by the practice of virtue. However, as Jesus explains to Luisa, that means waiting for opportunities to exercise the virtue. For example, one cannot exercise the virtue of obedience if there is nothing to be obedient to. Or one cannot exercise the virtue of patience if the opportunity for patience does not present itself. This has been the way of sanctity until the time of Luisa. Jesus has revealed to her, and consequently to us, a new means of sanctity. The foundations of virtue must still be in place, so we still have to exercise virtue. However, according to what Jesus reveals to Luisa, every act performed in the Divine Will enables the soul to grow in sanctity, not because of what the soul is doing, but because of what Jesus does in the soul. The person who accepts the gift of living in the Divine Will, has been raised, by grace, to the eternal mode of prayer and action[44] (see explanation in chapter two). The various prayers that Jesus teaches, which are taught in this book, are often

[43] Piccarreta, L, Book of Heaven, Volume 13, September 14th, 1921.

[44] 'The eternal mode of prayer and action is how the soul operates when it has received the gift of Living in the Divine Will. Every act that is fused into the Divine Will is raised by grace from the temporal mode into God's eternal mode.

called 'acts.' For example, 'Act of Resignation to the Divine Will,' or 'Act of Abandonment to the Divine Will.' Consequently, every act that the soul does in the Divine Will enables it to grow in sanctity.

What is an act? An act can be something physical (the movement of the fingers as we type or text), something spiritual (a prayer, meditation, contemplation), something psychological (thinking, reading, watching something on tv, listening to an audio book). Provided these acts are not sinful, they can be fused into the Divine Will and enable our growth in the Divine Will.

It is not about doing something big, like launching a rocket into space, or winning a trophy. It must be borne in mind that these acts, albeit great in the sight of some people, all began in simplicity. The launching of the rocket begins with the movement of a pen on paper as a scientist starts the calculations. Indeed, it can begin with the thought of flight into space. The winning of a trophy can begin with the athlete tying their laces. Each act, no matter how great or small, can begin with a relatively insignificant act. These apparently insignificant acts are the very things that can enable us to grow in holiness and grow in the eternal mode of prayer and action.

We live in a new era of holiness. Vatican 2 gave us teaching on how all of the people of God are called to the heights of holiness.[45] This is a central message of the council,

---

[45] See CCC, Article 2013.

and it directs us to the core principle of what it means to be a Catholic – to be holy.

Jesus repeats to Luisa that each time the soul does her acts in His Will (as opposed to the human will) the soul grows…

'She grows more and more before Me in wisdom, in goodness, power and beauty.' [46]

The wisdom, goodness, power and beauty, that are the Divine life, grow in the creature as she undertakes her acts in the Divine Will. Note that the growth is 'before Me,' i.e. Christ. Jesus grew in wisdom and statute before men and God. We grow before Christ. The journey is hidden from others, which is normal for a soul growing in the Divine Will. We look to two of our models, Our Lady and Luisa, two very hidden souls. The life of the Divine Will is seen by God, not by others. Indeed, others may look at us and see evil. Why? Because the bright, blazing light of the Divine Will that is growing in the soul of the one in the Divine Will can be offensive to the soul that is walking in darkness. When a soul loves darkness, they hate the blazing light of God's Divine Will, and they might consider you an evil person for revealing the truth of who they are to themselves. This is not necessarily the universal experience, but it can be

---

[46] Piccarreta, L, Book of Heaven, Volume 13, September 14th, 1921.

the experience. One soul might respond in this way, another soul might respond by desiring what you have.

In Ezekiel 3:3 the prophet is told to *'eat the scroll'* and he does so. He does this in order to provide himself with nourishment and to nourish the people of Israel who are living in exile. God always wants to feed his people. Now, as the world plummets into ever deepening sin and darkness, God wants to nourish His chosen people.

'In fact, as she keeps repeating her acts in my Will, she takes as many bites of wisdom, of goodness, etc; and the soul grows from that food with which she feeds herself.' [47]

It can be seen from the words of Jesus that the soul in the Divine Will 'grows' from each act she performs. Each act is a bite of wisdom, goodness, beauty, and each time the soul performs an act in the Divine Will, she is being nourished on the wisdom of God, the goodness of God, the beauty of God. This is because God is the only nourishment for the soul, the only food, the only drink. So as the soul does its acts in the Divine Will, it is being continuously nourished from God's own person.

---

[47] Piccarreta, L, Book of Heaven, Volume 13, September 14th, 1921.

Apply logic to the scenario. When a person has what we might call a 'traditional diet,' they will take as food the meat of an animal. It could be a cow, sheep, lamb, fish, to name but a few. These animals nourish the flesh, the physical part of our being. Without this food (plus the vegetables, fruit and carbohydrates) the person will soon become malnourished and might die. This same scenario applies to the soul. The soul is the spiritual part of a person. As a spiritual part of us, the only way it can be nourished is via the spirit. I cannot be nourished from the spiritual part of other people, they do not have the capacity to feed my soul. They can talk to me about God via retreats, conversations, conferences, and such like, but the One feeding the soul through such experiences is God.

For those souls who are in the Divine Will, we feed through our acts, which are not human acts performed with the human will, but eternal and infinite acts performed with the Divine Will, in the eternal mode of prayer and action. Again, it must be noted that only the soul who has given God her fiat and is thus living in the Divine Will is able to eat from the Divine Wisdom in this way. The eternal mode of prayer and action is only available to those who are giving God their fiat and allowing God's Divine Will to be the operative Will in their soul.

Each act in the Divine Will is formed by God in eternity.

'Even before there is a word on my tongue, Behold, LORD, You know it all... Your eyes have seen my unformed substance; And in Your book were all written The days that were ordained for me, When as yet there was not one of them.'

Psalm 139:4, 16

The acts in the Divine Will are the outpouring of God:

I continued my acts in the Divine Fiat, and feeling that I was not doing them well, I prayed my Celestial Mama to come to my help, that I might be able to follow that Supreme Volition which She had loved so much, and from which She recognized having received all Her glory and the height at which She finds Herself. [48]

I would invite the reader to take note that we often call on Our Lady's help during a crisis, like the sickness of a family member, or the near death of the same. A financial crisis, a journey, a disaster like an earthquake or severe storm (hurricane for example). There are many others, but it is to demonstrate that it is such exterior problems that cause us to invoke the help of Our Lady either directly, or by praying the rosary, a novena, etc. On the other hand, Luisa was doing her acts in the Divine Will and called on the help of Our Lady. Her motive? That she might follow the Supreme Volition for the glory Our Lady received. Part of this journey in the Divine Will is to 'follow' in the acts of those

[48] Luisa Piccarreta, Book of Heaven, Volume 23, December 1st, 1927.

who have gone before us, this will be further explained in the chapter on 'Rounds.'

Luisa did not feel she was doing her acts very well and prays for Our Lady's assistance. Ponder this well. When I talk to someone who is striving to live their life in the Divine Will and they reveal how inconsistent they are with their daily acts or fusing themselves in the Divine Will, or their struggle to 'remember', it is often that they feel they are failing, and they try to be more resolved to do better. Can there be a little bit of pride or ego in this attitude of 'striving to do better'? Luisa shows us that really we need to be calling out for heaven's help, and she turns to Our Lady. She does not try and solve the issue herself – she turns to heaven. May I propose to the reader that as they grow in the Divine Will and experience the resultant struggles associated with the interior life of prayer and action, that instead of struggling on alone, that they turn to Our Lady for help.

Our Lady, Help of Christians, pray for us.

Luisa continues:

But while I was thinking of this, my lovable Jesus, moving in my interior, told me: "My daughter, all the acts of my Queen Mother, done in my Will, are all in waiting, for they want the retinue of the acts of the creature done in It. So, in everything you do in my Volition, it is these acts that come to your help; even more, they line up around you to administer to you - some the light, some the grace, some the sanctity, and some the very act that you do, so as to have the retinue of these noble, holy and divine acts." [49]

Jesus comes to teach Luisa after her prayer for the help of Our Lady. It is Jesus who teaches us about the gift of living in the Divine Will. However, he teaches Luisa that all of the acts of Our Lady, done in His Will, are in waiting. Although these acts are done primarily for God's glory, they are also done for you. Every act that Our Lady did was done for your benefit.

It is also to be noted that each act in the Divine Will is alive, they are not dead like the usual acts performed in the human will, they contain God's own life. Each act contains a Divine Life. Consequently, the acts can 'wait.' The acts of Our Lady await the acts of the creature that are done in the Divine Will, and it is Our Lady's acts that come to the help of the creature, lining up around each child of the Divine Will.

Each act administers something different to the soul in the Divine Will. Some administer light to you. Ponder this mystery. One act of Our Lady, perhaps her cooking in the house of Nazareth whilst Jesus and Joseph were busy doing carpentry, that act which was performed 2,000 years ago, is administering light to you in the present moment. Another will administer grace, yet another sanctity. Each of these

[49] Luisa Piccarreta, Book of Heaven, Volume 23, December 1st, 1927.

acts of Our Lady will administer something different to your soul. Each act that Our Lady performed when she was on earth is awaiting our own act in the Divine Will so that her act can administer light, grace, and sanctity to us.

Yet, there is another twist in the mystery. According to the above teaching of Jesus, Our Lady's acts could even minister to your soul your own act. Don't forget, that act you performed is not just your act, it contains an outpouring of God, it is alive with a Divine life.

'These acts are the outpouring of God; and as He feeds them to the creature, she is filled so much that, unable to contain them, she pours them out again and gives her divine acts to her Creator. Therefore, they form the greatest glory which the creature can give to the One who created her.' [50]

Each act that the creature does in the Divine Will is an outpouring of God. The act is first formed by God in eternity, he fuses it into the soul at the time the soul is about to perform the act, the act is performed by the creature in the Divine Will, and it is then taken to heaven by the angels and placed around the throne of God. It could be a prevenient act, a present act, a heroic act, meditating on the Hours of the Passion, etc. Any apparently insignificant act, because it is fused into the Divine Will, was formed in

---

[50] Piccarreta, L., Book of Heaven, Volume 23, December 1st, 1927.

eternity, and fused into my soul, before I carried it out in His Will. The act forms a new and perpetual Pentecost in the soul because it is an outpouring of God, which is the definition of the Pentecost found in Acts 2. The outpouring of the Holy Spirit in the form of tongues of fire, with Our Lady in the midst of the birth of the Church.

At the dawn of this new era of peace, here we are in Our Lady's presence, performing small, silent acts, that are filled with God. Acts that '*form the greatest glory which the creature can give to the One who created her.*'

Fiat!

7. The sole purpose of Creation.

'For since the creation of the world His invisible attributes, that is, His eternal power and divine nature, have been clearly perceived, being understood by what has been made.'

Romans 1:20

The teaching of Christ as revealed to Luisa provides us with a clear picture of the dignity of the human person and our centrality in Creation:

'In all centuries there has always been some soul whom God has formed as centre of the whole Creation, and within her our love leaned and our life palpitated and obtained the purpose of the whole Creation.' [51]

God has always chosen a soul in whom to centre His Creation, and with whom He could lean His infinite and eternal love. Such souls often suffer a great deal as the bright light of God's eternal and infinite love is in stark contrast to the love they would bear witness to in the world. Indeed, in

---

[51] Piccarreta, L., Book of Heaven, Volume 29, October 20th, 1931.

Luisa's writings she often pleads with Jesus to take her to heaven because she so longs to be perpetually with God.

I also remind the reader that the teachings of Christ on the Gift of Living in the Divine Will are regarded by Him as the science of sciences because they are the most revered study of the interior life of God. They also tell us about the history and purpose of Creation from the perspective of the One who created everything. As well as the science and knowledge of God, these writings also teach us about the knowledge of the human person, the purpose for our creation and our centrality in the cosmos. We are not just a speck of dusty on a meaningless planet, but an absolutely necessity in keeping the entire universe in existence:

'It is by means of these centres (of Creation) that the whole Creation is maintained, and that the whole world still exists, otherwise, it would have no reason to exist because the life and the cause of everything would be missing.' [52]

God created man as the centre of his Creation and if we were missing, the world would cease to exist. Again, this is in stark contrast with some modern thinking. Some groups maintain that if mankind did not exist on the earth all of

---

[52] Piccarreta, L., <u>Book of Heaven, Volume 29,</u> October 20th, 1931.

nature would flourish, overtaking the cities and man-made inventions (road, railways) and reclaiming the earth for its own purpose. However, the Creator tells us that the opposite is the case, were it not for the existence of man the entirety of Creation would no longer have a reason to exist because it finds its purpose through humanity.

'Therefore, there has not been one century, nor will there be, in which we will not choose souls dear to Us, more or less portentous, who will form the centre of Creation.'[53]

It is important to note how Jesus repeats the same statement again and again. He knew that there would be those who would seek to reduce or destroy the dignity of the human person through various means, so He clearly speaks the opposite language and reveals something of the incredible dignity of the creature that He created in His image and likeness. Consequently, He reveals very clearly that there has always been a soul on planet earth, who will be at the very centre of His Creation. Such a soul is 'more or less portentous'. By definition this means that they possess to a greater or lesser extent, the ability to achieve unexpected, effective results and extraordinary, miraculous powers through their work.

Furthermore:

---

[53] Piccarreta, L., Book of Heaven, Volume 29, October 20th, 1931.

'Now, you must know that these souls have been chosen by Our Divine Being in each century as centre of all creation.' [54]

This teaches us of our beautiful vocation as human beings and where God has placed us in the Universe. God reveals to us that human beings are at the very heart, the centre of His creation. Plus, He gives us a deeper revelation that in every century since Adam was in the garden of Eden there has always been a soul who God gave this grace to of being the centre of Creation. Consequently, humanity is not randomly on a rock circling a hot ball of gas on one of trillions of galaxies. When viewed from God's revelation, humanity is at the centre of creation. That has been the case for six thousand years since God created Adam.

Then Jesus speaks to Luisa, revealing to her a startling truth about her vocation:

'Now, in this century, We have chosen you as centre of all Creation…' [55]

Here we have it revealed to us that in the 20th century, for at least the duration of her life, Luisa was at the centre of all

---

[54] Piccarreta, L., Book of Heaven, Volume 29, October 20th, 1931.

[55] Piccarreta, L., Book of Heaven, Volume 29, October 20th, 1931.

Creation. She was the central point of the entire created universe, and this was for a given purpose which was in order to make known what it is due to God's Will so that we could long for it and call it to reign in our midst.

Now that we have laid down some groundwork, we can study the teaching of Jesus regarding the purpose of Creation, knowing that the human creature occupies the central point:

'Now, while I was fusing myself in the Holy Divine Volition in order to requite God in love for everything He had done in Creation for love of creatures, a thought was telling me that it was not necessary to do that; that this way of praying was not pleasing to my Jesus; that these are inventions of my mind.' [56]

This problem of Luisa's can often be a problem in prayer, especially for the contemplative, but even for those who have not yet proceeded from vocal, petitionary prayer, to that of contemplation. One can feel that one is wasting one's time. However, Jesus reassures Luisa, and even completely contradicts her:

And my always lovable Jesus, moving in my interior, told me: "My daughter, you must know that this way of praying – that is, to requite

---

[56] Piccarreta, L., Book of Heaven, Volume 18, August 9th, 1925.

God in love for all the things created by Him – is a divine right, and it enters the first duty of the creature." [57]

To requite is to make an appropriate return for a favour or service, to respond with love or affection. Jesus teaches us that to respond with love for the beauty of creation is the first duty of the creature. It is also a Divine right. Ponder over all of those human rights that some people like to constantly remind one another about; those 'equal' rights that are constantly trumpeted by various groups. Well, for God to receive a return of love for His creation is a Divine right – the most important right of all. It very much 'turns the tables' on us because we can be consumed with OUR various rights, without realizing that the one who created all things has a far greater right. However, thanks to Jesus revealing this truth to Luisa, we can satisfy this Divine right on behalf of all creatures of all time.

Jesus teaches Luisa:

'The Creation was made for love of man; even more, Our love was so great that, had it been necessary, We would have created as many heavens, as many suns, stars, seas, earths, plants and all the rest, for as many creatures as were to come to the light of this world, so that each one of them might have a Creation for herself, a universe of her own.' [58]

---

[57] Piccarreta, L., Book of Heaven, Volume 18, August 9th, 1925.

[58] Piccarreta, L., Book of Heaven, Volume 18, August 9th, 1925.

This is a very interesting statement from Jesus. First, that the entire creation was created for love of us. Jesus then reveals that He would have created a universe for each individual. Saint Peter Chrysologus, Bishop of Ravenna who died in the year 450, in his sermon on the Sacrament of Christ's incarnation, said:

'Why then, man, are you so worthless in your own eyes and yet so precious to God? Why render yourself such dishonour when you are honoured by him? Why do you ask how you were created and do not seek to know why you were made? Was not this entire visible universe made for your dwelling? It was for you that the light dispelled the overshadowing gloom; for your sake was the night regulated and the day measured, and for you were the heavens embellished with the varying brilliance of the sun, the moon and the stars. The earth was adorned with flowers, groves and fruit; and the constant marvellous variety of lovely living things was created in the air, the fields, and the seas for you, lest sad solitude destroy the joy of God's new creation. And the Creator still works to devise things that can add to your glory. He has made you in his image that you might in your person make the invisible Creator present on earth; he has made you his legate, so that the vast empire of the world might have the Lord's representative.'

These beautiful teachings remind us that we are the centre of God's creation, not just another creature standing on a rock circling one of countless stars. No, we are unique, and this is what God has revealed to us through the teachings of his Saints. Indeed, we are so unique that God chose one of us as a spectator of Creation:

'And, in fact, when everything was created, Adam was the only spectator of all Creation - he could enjoy all the good he wanted. And if We did not do so, it was because man could enjoy everything anyway, as if it were his own, even if others also might enjoy it.' [59]

Jesus teaches Luisa that the only human being who was the spectator of creation after it had come forth from His own Word, was the first man, Adam. Created roughly six thousand years ago, he would have been alive today but for his sin, and he could enjoy everything in creation. Not just everything on earth, but the entire universe. This is the situation of Adam before The Fall; a man who was fully alive, untainted by original sin, and in a beautiful communion of love with all three persons of the Trinity. His soul overflowing with the Divine Will, and as the only rational creature in the physical creation, he can enjoy it as his own.

In the following quote Jesus teaches Luisa about the purpose of creation. He teaches her about what man owes to God for what God has given man:

---

[59] Piccarreta, L., Book of Heaven, Volume 18, August 9th, 1925.

'So, given all this – that in all created things God bound His love toward each creature – hers was the duty to requite God with her little love, with her gratitude, with her 'thank You' to the One who had done so much for her. Not requiting God in love for everything He has done for man in Creation, is the first fraud that the creature makes against God; it is to usurp His gifts without even recognizing where they come from, and the One who has loved her so much.'[60]

Jesus reveals something about creation that we have to be very aware of for this era in history. In all created things, God has bound His love toward each creature. There is a bond of love between us and God that is to be found in all creation. Note, this is not us loving creation as a last end. We do not love creation for its own sake. We love creation, recognising God's love in everything. We see God revealed to us in creation and find a bond of love that God has placed there. If you like, it is a covenant of love that is found in creation. Our sole duty in this is to requite God with our little love, with our "thank you." Otherwise, it is fraudulent. In the history of the world, up to the time of Luisa, only one creature has ever fulfilled this duty… the Blessed Virgin Mary:

'Therefore, this is the first duty of the creature, and this duty is so indispensable and important, that She who took to heart all Our glory,

---

[60] Piccarreta, L., Book of Heaven, Volume 18, August 9th, 1925.

Our defence, Our interest, did nothing but go around through all the spheres, from the smallest to the greatest thing created by God, in order to impress Her requital of love, of glory, of thanksgiving, for all and in the name of all human generations. Ah! yes, it was precisely my Celestial Mama who filled Heaven and earth with the requital for everything that God had done in Creation.'[61]

Jesus is teaching us about the Blessed Virgin Mary, the Queen of the Divine Will, Queen of Peace. He tells us how Our Lady 'took to heart all our glory.' She could do this because she had the gift of Living in the Divine Will from the moment of her Immaculate Conception. Hence, she could give God a perfect return of glory for the entirety of her existence. This is the primary reason for our creation, the glory of God. Our Lady took this to heart and impressed her 'requital of glory' for all, and in the name of all – including you and me. Once again, requital means 'to make an appropriate return'. Let us ponder this briefly. God created you. You exist. You clearly have reason, intellect, wisdom, and various abilities. These abilities have not been given to you for your own glory, in contrast with the celebrities, sports stars, etc, who largely have a tendency to seek their own glory. In all honesty, this is arguably one of the hardest things about the spiritual life, to do things purely for the glory of God. Our own ego wants to be fed and nourished by the fake glory that we might receive from

---

[61] Piccarreta, L., *Book of Heaven, Volume 18,* August 9th, 1925.

others. However, we were created for the glory of God and until we give (requite) to God his glory, we will remain somewhat 'empty'. Having read the testimonies of a few 'celebrities' who became Christians, they would testify that in spite of being on a stage or in an arena, receiving glory from their fellow human beings, they felt 'empty' afterwards.

Contrast that experience with souls who serve God. They will testify how they are 'filled' with the Divine Presence. They will reference the peace that filled them, the love that overwhelmed them.

Our Lady is the first soul to requite God during her entire human life for all of creation, recognising the beautiful gift that God has given to humanity. Now we have an opportunity to do the same. However, first Jesus teaches us about what He did on our behalf:

"After Her came my Humanity, which fulfilled this duty so sacrosanct, in which the creature had so very much failed, and rendered my Celestial Father benevolent toward guilty man. So, these were my prayers, and those of my inseparable Mama. Don't you want, then, to repeat my very prayers? Even more, this is why I have called you into my Will – that you may associate yourself with Us, and follow and repeat Our acts."[62]

---

[62] Piccarreta, L., Book of Heaven, Volume 18, August 9th, 1925.

Again, let us consider what Jesus is teaching us as Luisa writes:

So I tried, as much as I could, to go around through all created things, to give to my God the requital of love, of glory, of gratitude, for everything He had done in Creation. I seemed to see in all created things the requital of love of my Empress Mama and of my beloved Jesus. This requital formed the most beautiful harmony between Heaven and earth, and bound the Creator to the creature. Each requital of love was a key, a little sonata of enrapturing celestial music. [63]

In the first chapter Jesus talks about how the nine excesses of love are the prelude to all the other teachings on the Divine Will. The prelude is a reference to the first part of a piece of music. In the above quote He is revealing to Luisa how the requital of love that the creature has an obligation to give, is a piece of heavenly music:

And my sweet Jesus added: "My daughter, all created things were nothing other than an act of Our Will that issued them; nor can they move, or change the effects, the position or the office which each of them received by its Creator. They are nothing other than mirrors in which man was to admire the reflections of the qualities of his Creator: in some the power, in some the beauty, in other created things the goodness, the immensity, the light, etc. In sum, each created thing preaches to man

---

[63] Piccarreta, L., Book of Heaven, Volume 18, August 9th, 1925.

the qualities of its Creator, and with mute voices they tell him how much I love him."[64]

All created things are mirrors in which man can admire the reflections of the qualities in the Creator. For example, the bright light of the sun reflects God's brightness, because *'God is light'* (1 John 1:5). Also, the more scientists gaze up at the universe and aim their telescopes into the distance, the more they are confronted with 'infinity'. They are looking into infinity, a bit like a person who is standing on a boat and looks 'at' the sea without realising that they are actually looking 'into' the sea. In this last sentence we consider two invisible attributes of God in creation: in the universe we see a mirror of God's infinity, in the blue sea we see an image of the contemplation of God. When we contemplate him, we not just gazing 'at' him, but 'into' him. Just like the soul gazing 'into' the sea.

Jesus continues to teach about the sun and our free will:

"Oh! if a sun had a free will and could make two suns from one, four suns from two, what glory, what honour would it not give to its Creator, and how much glory also to itself? Yet, what the created things cannot do, because they are without a free will, and because they were created to serve man, man can do, because he was to serve God."[65]

---

[64] Piccarreta, L., Book of Heaven, Volume 18, August 9th, 1925.
[65] Piccarreta, L., Book of Heaven, Volume 18, August 9th, 1925.

Nothing else in creation has a free will except for human beings. We are the only rational creatures, the ones who have the ability to create (not out of nothing, but out of something). A bird might be seen 'creating' a nest, but it does it by instinct. No bird is ever trained to build that incredible nest. Only man can be trained and educated in order to create incredible works. This is all for the glory of God, but sadly most human achievements have been done for the self-glorification of man. However, here Jesus teaches Luisa about the purpose of creation. All created things were created to serve man. Man was created to serve God. Consequently, when you look at the entirety of creation you are looking at something that was created to serve you. You fulfil the purpose of creation by serving God, and creation looks to you as the one who somewhat bridges the gap. If we are not serving God, the purpose of creation remains frustrated. It cannot fulfil its purpose by glorifying God, because it does that through us.

Love centralised in man.

'So, all Our love was centralized in man, and this is why We placed all Creation at his disposal, all ordered around him – that man might make use of Our works like as many stairs and ways in order to come to Us, to know Us, and to love Us.'[66]

[66] Piccarreta, L., Book of Heaven, Volume 18, August 9th, 1925.

Again, this language needs to be pondered deeply. When you read above that '*we placed all creation at his disposal...that man might use of our works...to come to us..*' That is not just the creation that we see around us on earth. Creation is the entirety of the universe. Indeed, it is all that is visible and invisible. Ponder this; when Luisa was writing, scientists had no idea as to the vastness of the universe. Since the turn of the 21st century, and with the new technology that man has placed in satellites circling the globe, we are coming to a new appreciation of the unimaginable vastness of the universe. All of this, the entirety of it, was placed at Adam's disposal, and was for us to explore, to enjoy, and to give God a perfect return of glory. This perfect return can only be done with the gift of living in the Divine Will, because the creature uses God's own Will, God's own love, in order to love Him and bless Him for all that He has given to us.

We were meant to make use of the entire creation in order to come to God, to know Him, to love Him. It was not given to us to glorify man in some fashion. Indeed, atheistic evolutionary theory will not only completely disregard the creator and thus the fundamental purpose of creation, but it will also reduce man's existence to something insignificant. The earth becomes a 'little blue dot' in an insignificant solar system, in an insignificant galaxy. However, in the Divine Will teachings, the love of God was centralised in Adam, and the entire creation has been ordered around him.

Plus, all of those works are there for a most significant purpose, as a mirror in order for us to approach God. Know Him, love Him.

'But what is Our sorrow in seeing man below Our created things - even more, his beautiful soul, given by Us, transformed into ugliness by sin, and not only ungrown in good, but horrid to the sight? Yet, as if everything that was created for him were not enough to Our love, in order to preserve this free will, We gave him the greatest gift, which surpassed all other gifts: we gave him Our Will, as preserver, as antidote, as prevenience and help for his free will. So, Our Will placed Itself at his disposal, to give him all those aids which man might need. Our Will was given to him as primary life, and as the first act of all his works. Having to grow in grace and in beauty, he needed a Supreme Will, which would not only keep company with his human will, but would substitute for the operating of the creature.'[67]

This is the gift that God gave to Adam and Eve before the Fall, when they were filled with the Divine Life. It enabled them to gift God a perfect return of glory for His Creation, and it was the primary life and first act of all that Adam and Eve would do. Sadly, they despised the gift and lost it:

'But this great gift also he despised and did not want to know. See, then, how Our Will enters the primary life of the creature; and as long

---

[67] Piccarreta, L., Book of Heaven, Volume 18, August 9th, 1925.

as It maintains Its first act, Its life, the creature grows always in grace, in light, in beauty; she preserves the bond of the first act of her creation, and We receive the glory of all created things, because they serve Our Will operating in the creature – the only purpose of all Creation. Therefore, I recommend to you – let Our Will be more than life for you, and the first act of all your actions.'[68]

Fiat!

[68] Piccarreta, L., Book of Heaven, Volume 18, August 9th, 1925.

8. Rounds of the Soul

'For the creation waits with eager longing for the revealing of the sons of God;'

Romans 8:16

Everything around us was created by God. All the stars, planets, galaxies, moons, asteroids, every plant, tree, flower, crop, insect, animal, cloud, etc. The list goes on. It was all created by God, and He holds everything in being by the power of His Word. He wills that we would reciprocate His love by a continuous act of love on our behalf, in His Divine Will. Indeed, Jesus explains to Luisa that this is an obligation of the soul:

"Know that each soul, during the whole course of her life, is obliged to love Me constantly, with no interval; and if she does not love Me always, she leaves as many voids in her soul for as many days, hours or minutes in which she has neglected to love Me. But no one will be able to enter Heaven if he has not filled these voids; and one will only be able to fill them by loving Me twice as much for the rest of his life; and if he does not arrive at doing this, he will fill them by dint of fire in Purgatory. Now, when you are deprived of Me, the privation of the beloved makes love double, and by this, you come to fill the voids that there are present in your soul."[69]

---

[69] Piccarreta, L., Book of Heaven, Volume 4. September 4th, 1901.

When we make a journey in the interior life by either prayer, reading spiritual works, or attending religious services (Mass for example), there is an opportunity for us to grow in our knowledge of self and our knowledge of God. The above quote reveals to us a little about us, and a little about God. Firstly, they reveal that we were created to love God from the first moment of our conception and for all eternity, in every moment. This reveals something about us and about God. It tells us that God created us for love, and therefore that he is love. It tells us that God loves us at every moment of our existence, and prior to our existence because he loved us 'before the creation of the world' (Ephesians 1:4,5). Knowledge of God feeds our knowledge of self, a bit like looking into a mirror. Consequently, we discover that our lack of loving God has left our soul empty, a huge void. The way you feel today is the consequence of that void. There is only one way to fill that void, by loving God.

God helps us in this by offering us this beautiful gift and all of the teaching that goes with it from Luisa Piccarreta. We learn that when we are deprived of God's presence the voids are filled. That deprivation could be by not being able to access the Blessed Sacrament for a period of time; it could be by being deprived of consolations, or by a trial, a dryness. There a multiple ways that God can cause the soul to be expanded and the voids filled. Either way, God does not want us suffering in purgatory (which is a waste of time for us according to Saint Therese of Lisieux).

There is also another void, that of the glory owed by human beings to God. We were all created to give God a perfect return of glory from the first moment of our existence. Clearly we have not done that, so there is a void in the glory that is owed to God by human creatures.

After this, He seemed to transport me outside of myself, and He made me see the multitude of the peoples, and the good which they can do, but do not, and therefore the glory which God must receive, but does not. All afflicted, Jesus added: "My beloved, my Heart burns for the honour of my glory and the good of souls. For each good they omit, my glory and their souls receive a void." [70]

With the gift of living in the Divine Will, God has given us the opportunity, the grace, and the power to fill this void, not just for ourselves, but for all human creatures of all time. One way of filling up these voids is by something known as 'rounds of the soul'. By doing 'rounds' in the Divine Will, the soul fills up the void in the glory owed by creatures to God. God then fills up the void in the human soul by His grace. The rounds in the Divine Will give God a perfect, eternal and infinite return of love and glory, as is befitting.

---

[70] Piccarreta, L., Book of Heaven, Volume 4, September 4th, 1901.

What is a 'round' of the soul?

In the area of Italy where Luisa lived, Corato, the people have a wander at some point during their day. They go around the houses and coffee shops, greeting one another, having some time together, being friendly. Jesus uses this very human activity to introduce the soul to the rounds of the soul. He wants us to wander around Creation, past, present and future in order to reciprocate the love that He has placed in everything. Fr Joseph Iannuzzi comments that the soul's acts of going throughout creation to love God as the centre of all that he made and did for mankind, are referred to by Luisa as the Rounds in Creation.[71] Jesus further explains:

'My daughter, Our love in Creation was exuberant, but always towards man. In each created thing, We put so many acts of love for as many times that the creature must make use of that created thing. Our Divine Fiat, which maintains the equilibrium in all of Creation and is the perennial life of it, when It sees that the creature is about to serve itself of the light of the sun, It puts Our love in function to make Our love be encountered in the light that the creature receives. If the creature drinks water, Our love makes itself be encountered to say to the creature while it drinks: 'I love you'. If the creature breathes air, Our love repeatedly says to it: 'I love you'. If it walks on the earth, Our love says

---

[71] Fr Joseph Iannuzzi, The Gift of Living in the Divine Will in the Writings of Luisa Piccarreta: An Inquiry into the Early Ecumenical Councils, and into Patristic, Scholastic and Contemporary Theology, Missionaries of the Holy Trinity, 2013, page 105.

to in under its steps: 'I love you'. There is nothing that the creature takes, touches and sees, in which Our love does not make its happy encounter with the creature by saying to it: 'I love you', to give it love. But do you know what the cause is of so much insistence of Our love? So that We receive the encounter of the creature's love in each thing that it takes. Therefore, infinite love wanted to encounter finite love and form one alone, to put the equilibrium of His (God's) love in the creature. And since the creature serves itself of created things without even thinking that Our love goes to meet it in the things that it takes to make it hear Our repeated chorus 'I love you, I love you', and serves itself without giving a glance to Him who sends the created things to it, the creature's love remains unbalanced, because not meeting with Our love, the creature's love loses the equilibrium and remains disordered in all of its acts, because it has lost the Divine equilibrium and the strength of the love of its Creator. So, be attentive with your exchange of love in order to make reparation to Me for so much coldness of creatures."[72]

In this excerpt from Luisa's writings, Jesus reveals to us, the *creature*, that He has placed his love in all created things. He reveals to us that we can encounter the love of the Trinity in everything. However, God requires a reciprocation of this same love. When we return the love of God, or place our love, with the gift of living in the Divine Will, in those same created things, then God receives an encounter with

[72] Piccarreta, L., Book of Heaven, Volume 28, April 1st, 1930.

our love. This is a description of the rounds of creation. There are also rounds of redemption and sanctification.

With the rounds of redemption the creature can follow the different moments of the story of redemption, for example the Immaculate Conception of the Blessed Virgin Mary, and place its 'I love you, I adore you' in her conception. The creature can then follow the acts of Our Lady, Jesus, the New Testament stories, the mysteries of the Rosary, placing its 'I love you' in all of the different acts and events.

The same can happen for the rounds of sanctification which involves the movement of the Holy Spirit in the life of the Church. The soul can place its 'I love you' in the lives of the all the Saints, the teachings on the Divine Will (one can place 'I love you' in every word that Luisa writes), the coming era of peace, the purification of the Church.

In all of this we remember:

'We love, because He first loved us.'

1 John 4:19

Further quoting Fr Joseph Iannuzzi, 'In each round the soul operating in the Divine Will gives God an infinite, eternal, perfect, return of love which is: 'Transtemporal (extending the souls acts to all things throughout the universe), universal (sanctifies all creatures, rational and irrational), and multiplication (multiplies its divine acts in all things).' [73]

I remind the reader that this book is an introduction to the Gift of Living in the Divine Will. Please do not expect to understand all of these different prayers and spiritual exercises at the first reading. As we ruminate and masticate on the words of Christ, the same words will find a good place in our soul and in a relatively short space of time we will find ourselves doing prevenient acts, actual acts, rounds, etc. It will not just be second nature, but it will be like being caught in a flowing river from dawn to dusk.

One of my favourite ways of doing the rounds is through the rosary; to place 'I love you' in each of the mysteries of Christ's life but walking with Our Lady. This also involves taking the acts of Christ's life, and Our Lady's, and making them one's own, as in the practice of prayer in the Divine Will. This is all done for the glory of God.

"My daughter, true love, accompanied even by the words 'I love You', is never tiring to Me, because I, being a complex of love and a continuous act of love who never ceases to love, when I find my love in the creature, I find Myself. The sign that the love of the creature is part of my love is when the creature's love is continuous. An interrupted love is not a sign of Divine Love. At the most, it can be a love of

---

[73] Fr Joseph Iannuzzi, The Gift of Living in the Divine Will in the Writings of Luisa Piccarreta: An Inquiry into the Early Ecumenical Councils, and into Patristic, Scholastic and Contemporary Theology, Missionaries of the Holy Trinity, 2013, page 109.

circumstances, or a love of interest, which, once these cease, love ceases. Even the words 'I love You, I love You' are nothing other than the air that my love produces in the creature, which, condensed in the creature, produces many flashes of lights towards Him who the creature loves. And I, when I hear said 'I love You, I love You', do you know what I say? 'My daughter is flashing lights - in the air of her love towards Me, and one flash does not wait for the other.' And then, all the continuous acts (done in my Volition) are those that have the virtue to conserve, feed, and grow the Life of the creature." [74]

Fiat!

---

[74] Piccarreta, L., Book of Heaven, Volume 28, October 12th, 1930.

9. 'Fiat Voluntas Tua'

"Promise to be faithful to me and I shall pour into you many graces that will cause you to marvel.
I have great designs on you, but only if you correspond and conform to My Will.
I shall delight in making you a perfect image of Me.
You shall imitate Me from My birth to My death.
Do not have any doubt about succeeding,
because I will teach you how it can be done a little at a time."[75]

Perhaps the most important line in this quote is the first one. The Lord calls on us to be faithful to Him:

'Those who are with Him are the called and chosen and faithful.'

Revelation 17:14

This faithfulness can be misunderstood. God does not choose the perfect, he perfects the chosen. He just invites us to hear his word and let it find a place in our hearts; '*I will put My law within them and write it on their heart.*' (Jeremiah 31:33). He wants to write His teaching on your heart. With that in

---

[75] Piccarreta, L., Book of Heaven, Volume 1, page 4.

mind, let us read about the three Fiats and what Jesus wants to write on your heart regarding where the Church and the world are today.

Jesus speaks to Luisa about the three Fiats which are found in the Latin version of Sacred Scripture:

Genesis 1:3, '*Fiat lux*' (Let there be light)

Luke 1:38, '*Fiat mihi*' (Let it be done to me)

Matthew 6:10, '*Fiat voluntas tua*' (Your will be done)

The Latin word 'fiat' is translated in God's Word as 'let there be' or a similar short phrase. It is understood to be a word of command, a word of authority. In Luisa's teaching Jesus talks about how the Fiat is alive:

"My daughter, the Fiat is all full of Life - even more, It is Life Itself, and this is why all lives and all things come from within the Fiat." [76]

Jesus teaches Luisa about the power of each Fiat. For example, in respect of the Fiat of Creation, Jesus tells Luisa, "*Creation came out from my 'Fiat' therefore, in each created thing one can see the mark of the Fiat.*" [77] Could this mark be associated with DNA, which is found in all created things? As with the word 'FIAT' there are four letters that constitute DNA

[76] Piccarreta, L., Book of Heaven, Volume 12, January 17th, 1921.
[77] Piccarreta, L., Book of Heaven, Volume 12, January 17th, 1921.

which are A, C, G, T. Indeed, the chemical that constitutes the letter C, Cytosine, is derived from the Greek 'kytos' meaning a 'hollow' or 'receptacle' from which we get the word for 'cell'. The cell was first introduced to the language of science by a British scientist called Robert Hooke, who on examining some dead cork under a microscope noticed the order of the shapes and thought of them as being like the cells of monks in a monastery. These cells were called the 'basic functional units of living things', and it is this word which gives us one of the four letters of DNA.[78] Consequently, whereas Jesus tells us that the FIAT is life itself, science has shown us that DNA is the basic functional unit of living things.

Then there is the Fiat Mihi of Redemption:

'Redemption came out from the 'Fiat Mihi' of my dear Mama, pronounced in my Volition and carrying the same power of my Creative 'Fiat.' Therefore, there is nothing in Redemption which does not contain the mark of the 'Fiat Mihi' of my Mama. Even my very Humanity, my steps, words and works were marked by Her 'Fiat Mihi.' My pains, my wounds, my thorns, my Cross, my Blood, had the mark of Her 'Fiat Mihi,' because things carry the mark of the origin from which they come. My origin in time was the 'Fiat Mihi' of the

---

[78] A search on Google or Bing will reveal all of this wonderful information about DNA.

Immaculate Mama; therefore all of my works carry the mark of Her 'Fiat Mihi.' So, Her 'Fiat Mihi' is in each Sacramental Host; if man rises again from sin, if the newborn is baptized, if Heaven opens to receive souls, it is the 'Fiat Mihi' of my Mama that marks everything, follows everything, and from It everything proceeds.' [79]

We can see that whereas everything in Creation is marked by the Fiat Lux, everything in Redemption is marked by the Fiat Mihi. The Fiat is not just an empty word, it is powerful. Jesus declares to Luisa:

'Oh, power of the Fiat! It rises every instant; It multiplies, and It becomes life of all goods.' [80]

We live in the era of the third Fiat, the '*Fiat voluntas tua*'. When Jesus was on earth, he taught his disciples a prayer that we call the 'Lord's Prayer,' alternatively known as the Our Father. Jesus taught Luisa that he placed a prophecy in that prayer which in Latin reads 'fiat voluntas tua sicut in caelo et in terra'. That translates as 'Your Will be done on earth as it is in heaven'. Jesus teaches Luisa:

"Now I want to tell you why I asked for your 'Fiat' - your 'yes' in my Volition. I want the prayer which I taught – the 'Fiat Voluntas

---

[79] Piccarreta, L., Book of Heaven, Volume 12, *January 17th*, 1921.
[80] Piccarreta, L., Book of Heaven, Volume 12, *January 17th*, 1921.

Tua sicut in Coelo et in terra' (Your Will be done on earth as it is in Heaven)- this prayer of so many centuries, of so many generations – to have its fulfillment and completion. This is why I wanted another 'yes' in my Volition - another 'Fiat' containing the creative power. I want the 'Fiat' that rises every instant and multiplies in everyone. I want, in one soul, my own 'Fiat' which ascends to my throne and, by Its creative power, brings upon earth the life of the 'Fiat on earth as It is in Heaven'."[81]

Note that the third Fiat contains the same creative power and effects of the Fiats of Creation and Redemption. All three Fiats have the same power and effect, and Jesus has entrusted this power to the human soul:

It is exactly in the Fiat Voluntas Tua that the Divine Spirit will display His work. [82]

According to the catechism section on prayer, the Holy Spirit is 'the Master of the interior life'.[83] Consequently, the *fiat voluntas tua* is the interior grace given to the soul in the state of grace that raises it to the eternal mode of prayer and action, enabling the soul to render unto God the perfect glory on behalf of all creatures that God should have had from the moment of man's creation six thousand years ago.

---

[81] Piccarreta, L., Book of Heaven, Volume 12, January 17th, 1921.
[82] Piccarreta, L., Book of Heaven, Volume 17, May 17, 1925.
[83] CCC, Article 1995.

This is where the Holy Spirit shall display his work, and it is the crown and glory of creation, the crown and glory of all other forms of sanctity. The actualising of the third fiat will inaugurate the kingdom of the Divine Fiat in souls on earth, and by reciting this prayer for 2,000 years the Church has petitioned for this kingdom and prepared souls to receive it.

Jesus teaches Luisa the effects of this petitioning and what is really coming to earth. Whereas the world is currently seen as a place of sin, war, crime, disasters, storms, disease, sickness, death. Jesus tells us where we are really headed:

"Oh iniquitous world, you are doing all you can to cast Me from the face of the earth, to expel Me from society, from schools, from conversations, and from everything. You are scheming to destroy temples and altars, to destroy My Church and kill My ministers. Yet I am preparing for you an era of Love, the era of my third Fiat ! You will continue your efforts to banish Me, but I will confound you with Love. I will follow you from behind, I will appear ahead of you, to confound you with Love; and wherever you cast Me, there will I establish My Throne; and there will I reign even more than before, and in a much more astounding manner, so much so that you yourself will fall at the foot of My Throne, as if bound by the force of My Love."[84]

[84] Piccarreta, L., Book of Heaven, Volume 12, February 8th, 1921.

The three purifications.

The coming era of love won't just happen. In order for humanity to be made ready for what God is going to give to us, there is the necessity of a purification. Just as in the natural order, if a person is preparing for a special occasion, they will clean themselves with a wash, a shower perhaps a bath, and then wear something special, in the same way God must cleanse, purify His people and prepare us for this era by clothing us in His grace. A purification is needed.

Just as there are three Fiats, and we are in the era of the third. So, there are three purifications, and we are in the era of the third one:

"My beloved daughter, I want to let you know the order of My Providence. Every two thousand years I have renewed the world. In the first two thousand years I renewed it with the Deluge; in the second two thousand I renewed it with My coming upon earth when I manifested my Humanity, from which, as if from many fissures, My Divinity shone forth. The good ones and the very Saints of the following two thousand years have lived from the fruits of my Humanity and, in drops, they have enjoyed my Divinity. Now we are around the third two thousand years, and there will be a third renewal. This is the reason for the general confusion: it is nothing other than the preparation of the third renewal. If in the second renewal I manifested what My Humanity did and suffered, and very little of what My Divinity was operating, now, in this third renewal, after the earth will be purged and a great part of the current generation destroyed, I will be even more

generous with creatures, and I will accomplish the renewal by manifesting what My Divinity did within My Humanity; how My Divine Will acted with My human will; how everything remained linked within Me; how I did and redid everything, and how even each thought of each creature was redone by Me, and sealed with my Divine Volition." [85]

What will this third renewal consist of? Wars, storms, viruses. The storms will increase in magnitude, and we are seeing this. There will be earthquakes that will destroy entire cities. However, the big chastisement or purification will be by fire. Just as God purified the world by a flood around 4,000 years ago, and His blood 2,000 years ago, now He is preparing to purify the world by fire.

'But by His word the present heavens and earth are being reserved for fire, kept for the day of judgment and destruction of ungodly men.'

1 Peter 3:7

Again in the prophet Zechariah 13:8, 9:

"It will come about in all the land,"

Declares the LORD,

"That two parts in it will be cut off and perish;

---

[85] Piccarreta, L., Book of Heaven, Volume 12, January 29th, 1919.

But the third will be left in it.
And I will bring the third part through the fire,
Refine them as silver is refined,
And test them as gold is tested.
They will call on My name,
And I will answer them;
I will say, 'They are My people,'
And they will say, 'The LORD is my God.'"

A potential two thirds, or the greater part of the current generation, will be purged from the earth by fire. This is because God wants to establish the Kingdom of His Divine Will on the earth, whereby only His Will will be the operative one in the human soul. Thus, a perfect unity of spirit will reign on earth. However, how can that perfect unity and peace be established if there are souls who want to continue doing their own will, with all of the destruction such a will causes. For example, imagine if 99% of the global population were living peacefully in God's Divine Will, but just a small 1% decided they wanted to continue 'doing as I see fit,' That 1% could be the drug dealers trying to cause immense misery, murder, evil. It could be the satanists, the abortionists murdering unborn children. It could be the sex traffickers and their evil trade. How could such people peacefully co-exist alongside the children of the Divine Will who have one desire, the perfect glory of God? They couldn't.

In the past, and even today, God has permitted evil doers to kill His children, and they became the wonderful martyrs of the Church. That was because the time had not yet come for His Kingdom to reign, the era of peace was not yet here. Now, the scenario is very different. The end of evil is upon us and God wishes to establish His peace on earth. This is the seventh millennium of human existence on earth, the sabbath day, the day which belongs to God, not to man. Essentially, the gift of living in the Divine Will is the martyrdom of martyrdoms, but that is because the human will is being put to rest in favour of the Divine Will. It is an interior martyrdom that must be lived out every moment of every day. So those who agree to this beautiful gift must live a day-to-day martyrdom. The martyrs of old only had one moment of martyrdom when they were put to death for their faith. The martyrs of the Divine Will have to perpetually live out the martyrdom of their human will.

The era of the Divine Fiat, the Divine Will, is upon the Church. Here are a few quotes from recent Popes and others regarding this new era:

'Dear young people, it is up to you to be the watchmen of the morning who announce the coming of the sun who is the Risen Christ![86]

My Immaculate heart will triumph...Russia will be converted... a period of peace will be granted to the world.'[87]

---

[86] Pope Saint John Paul 2, '*Message of the Holy Father to the youth of the world.* XVII World Youth Day, N.3 (cf. Isaiah 21:11-12)

I wish to tell you my secrets which, until now, I have not revealed to anyone because the hour of God had not yet sounded. God has wanted to bestow surprising graces upon souls which, in all the history of the world, he has not granted to anyone. [88]

"Oh the beauty of living in My Will! It so attracts Me that I will make all other sanctities under any aspect of virtue disappear in future generations, and I will make the sanctity of living in My Will reappear, which is not and shall not be a human sanctity, but a divine one. The sanctity (of those who possess it) will be so sublime that, like suns, they will eclipse the most beautiful stars of the saints of past generations. This is why I want to purge the earth: it is unworthy of these portents of sanctity." [89]

'In My all-encompassing vision, I see that these writings will be for My Church like a new sun that will arise within her midst, and her members, drawn by its blazing light, will seek to be transformed in this light and become spiritualized and divinized. Subsequently, by their having renewed the Church, they will transform the face of the earth.' [90]

Note, with this last prophecy, the writings are going to be the means for the transformation and divinisation of the members of the Church. It must be made clear that these writings were given by Christ to the Church. Therefore, it is absolutely imperative that all who seek to experience this transformation must remain in communion with the Church.

---

[87] Our Lady of Fatima, message of July 13th, 1917.

[88] Piccarreta, L., The Blessed Virgin Mary in the Kingdom of the Divine Will, Day 4.

[89] Piccarreta, L., Book of Heaven, Volume 22, November 20th, 1917.

[90] Piccarreta, L., Book of Heaven, Volume 16, February 10th, 1924.

The writings belong to the Body of Christ. Just like the Bible, which many read, but don't always realise that the Bible is the Church's book. It does not belong to those who are outside of the Church. They are obviously free to read it, but they cannot interpret it. It can only be interpreted in the Church. The same with Luisa, her writings must be lived and interpreted within the context of Church life. Also note that the Church will be transformed first, then the face of the earth. In Christ's words above, *'by their having renewed the Church…'* The children of the Divine Will are going to be the ones who renew the Church by their acts which are done in the eternal mode of prayer and action (the gift of living in the Divine Will). Only those who accept this grace can have their acts elevated into that eternal mode. Such acts will cause the renewal of the Church, then the *'transformation of the face of the earth.'* This will bring about the era of peace promised by Our Lady of Fatima.

Fiat!

10. The Call to the Creature

'Then the LORD God formed the man of dust from the ground,

and breathed into his nostrils the breath of life; and the man became a living person.'

Genesis 2:7

'Man is the summit of the Creator's work, as the inspired account expresses by clearly distinguishing the creation of man from that of the other creatures.'

Catechism of the Catholic Church, Article 343.

The title of Luisa's writings on the Gift of Living in the Divine Will has a long title given by Jesus on August 29th, 1926, in volume 19: *The Kingdom of the Divine Will among creatures. Book of Heaven. The call of the soul to the order, place and purpose for which God created it.*[91] Consequently, this chapter is devoted to the first man and God's Will at work in him. There is a lot of teaching in Luisa's diaries about this man, who is commonly known as Adam. The purpose of this

---

[91] There are different translations of this title, so I have taken this from the doctoral dissertation by Fr Joseph, *The Gift of Living in the Divine Will in the writings of Luisa Piccarreta,* Missionaries of the Holy Trinity, Inc. 2013.

chapter is to teach a little about the creation of this man so that we can see more clearly the call that God has placed on our lives, that call back to 'the order' for which we were created. By looking at the teaching of Christ on the Divine Will and how he created Adam, we can begin to appreciate that our current situation in life is very distant from what God originally planned for us. Thus, we will be able to respond to his grace in restoring to us what he originally established in creation. Our task is to respond to the grace and allow God to reorder our lives in order to conform to his great plan for us.

The first Adam and the last Adam

Catechism article 359, on the doctrine on creation, draws on the teaching of Saint Peter Chrysologus, who himself draws on Saint Paul:

St Paul tells us that the human race takes its origin from two men: Adam and Christ…The first man, Adam, he says, became a living soul, the last Adam a life-giving spirit. The first Adam was made by the last Adam from who he also received his soul, to give him life…The second Adam stamped his image on the first Adam when he created him.

It must be noted that this first man, Adam, was a real individual who lived approximately 6,000 years ago, not the tens of thousands of years currently proposed by erroneous scientific methods that are highly inaccurate and not based on truth. It has long been held that Adam was created around 4,000 years before Christ, that he was the first man, and that all humans descended from him. It is only in recent years that this revealed truth has been challenged. However, Luisa's doctrine was written whilst this truth was still held by the majority in the Church. Now, there is much confusion amongst theologians regarding the truth concerning Adam. Thankfully we can firmly uphold the truth of the matter thanks to the Catechism of the Catholic Church, (which was a fruit of Vatican 2), Luisa's writings, Sacred Scripture, Magisterial writings and Sacred Tradition.

'Before sinning, Adam possessed the complete life of My Divine Will in his soul. One can say that his soul was filled to the brim, to the extent of overflowing externally. Thus by virtue of my Will, his human will transfused light externally and emitted the fragrances of beauty, sanctity and purity, which engendered perfect health and strength. Such fragrances emanated from within Adam's will like many luminous clouds, while these exaltations so embellished his body that it was a delight to behold him so beautiful, vigorous, luminous, and perfectly healthy with an enrapturing grace." [92]

[92] Iannuzzi, Rev. Joseph, Leo, The Gift of Living in the Divine Will in the writings of Luisa Piccarreta, Missionaries of the Holy Trinity, Inc. 2013. P.36. Volume 24, July 7th, 1928.

The language used by Luisa (originating with Jesus) is beyond our grasp, because probably none of us have ever experienced what it would be like to be without the slightest stain of sin in the soul. Quite possibly, none of us have ever overflowed with the Divine Will, and had complete possession of the Divine Will causing perfect health, transfusing light external to our bodies, and having such perfection of sanctity and purity (the reader might well be slightly aggrieved at my 'sweeping generalisation' and you would be right to, it is not the sort of language I like to use). Jesus tells Luisa in another diary entry that Adam possessed such sanctity in God's one eternal act, that one simple act of Adam was more sanctified than all the acts of all the saints combined. It is a reasonably sure thing that what Adam possessed before the fall has somewhat eluded all but a tiny minority of the saints of the recent times, beginning with Luisa, and always recognising that Our Lady, The Blessed Virgin Mary, exceeded the sanctity of all creatures, visible and invisible.

This is the grace that Jesus wants to restore to us in this era. He wants to restore the pre-fall condition whereby the Divine life will overflow externally and our bodies will once again shine with the Divine life. The call of the creature to the 'order' for which he was created by God. This is the era in which we live, when the evil will finally be vanquished, the world purified, and the greatest army of saints the world has ever seen will finally be revealed. This is the call. So you need to meditate deeply on what Adam possessed, because it is likely that God wills that you one day possess such grace and glory.

To follow the call, we really need to know where we are heading, and the passage above gives us a good idea. There is more, always bearing in mind your call to the 'order, place and purpose for which you were created by God':

"Now, after I created everything, I formed man's human nature with my own creative hands. And just as I formed his bones, nerves and heart, so I centralized in him my love. After I clothed him with flesh, forming as though the most beautiful statue that no other artisan could ever make, I looked at him, and loved him with such uncontainable love that it overflowed, whence breathing on him I infused in him life."[93]

I remind the reader of Genesis 2:7:

'God formed man from the clay of the ground and breathed into him the breath of life…'

Jesus gives Luisa a deeper revelation of divinely revealed truth. The Church has always known that man was created by God, formed by him, and that before the fall the first

[93] Piccarreta, L. Book of Heaven, Volume 20. October 29th, 1926.

man (and woman) were in a state of sanctifying grace and attained to a certain degree of perfection. Luisa's writings enable us to dig a little deeper into the wellspring of that truth and show us the beauty and purpose of man's creation, and that God's love should 'overflow' from us. Whereas God breathed his breath into man in the garden of Eden, God wills that his breath be recognised as a fundamental component of our existence, not just a Pentecost event that happened 2,000 years ago. Rather, that breath of God, who is known as the Holy Spirit, is central to our lived reality as followers of Christ. It was central to the lived experience of the first man and woman, who were not alive until they were infused with the breath of God.

Yet, even though man is fully alive, God is not satisfied. The finite creature has always got more to receive from an infinite God, The well of divine revelations and experiences can never be exhausted,… not even close:

"But we, the Most Holy Trinity, were not satisfied. In an excess of love, we wanted to endow him with an intellect, a memory and a will that his creaturely capacity could contain. Thus we enriched him with all the perfections of our Divine Being. The fullness of our divinity was wholly intent on loving man, on pouring itself out into him. From the very first instant of his life Adam felt all the strength of our love, and from the depths of his heart, he expressed, with his own voice, his own love for his Creator…" [94]

---

[94] Piccarreta, L. Book of Heaven, Volume 20, October 29th, 1926.

Before those words are explicated, let us first examine what God is revealing to us in this passage. The intellect, memory and will were to be filled with the fullness of the divinity. According to Luisa, the intellect was the domain of the Logos (the pre-incarnate Christ), the memory was the domain of the Ruach (The Holy Spirit), and the will was the domain of the Father. Each person of the Trinity was going to fill a different faculty of Adam's soul, and each of those faculties was going to be enriched by that infusion of the Divine Being. Compare that with how things are at the moment you are reading this. The intellect can be filled with knowledge of medicine, science, music, literature, art, food, etc. However, these are all created! They are not the Creator. Our intellect is filled with that which has been created instead of He who created. Whereas our soul was intended to be filled with heaven, it is filled with earthly things. Intended for gold, it is filled with dust. Intended for riches, it is empty in its poverty.

The same applies for the memory. It was meant to be filled with the love of God personified, the Holy Spirit, known in the Old Testament as the Ruach (the Hebrew word for spirit – read the 'ch' at the end as in 'chemistry'). His domain was the memory, so that every memory the person would have would be of the love of God. Imagine the beauty of that. The recall of years ago would be nothing but experiences of God's love. No trauma, no painful memories, no bullying, manipulation, worry, fear. No death to remember, nor broken relationships, or breakdowns in life. The only memory would be how God has showered his love into your life from the moment of your conception for your entire existence. That was the original intention before Adam failed his test. The memory completely filled with the Holy Spirit. No voids in the memory allowing for any suffering, pain, difficult, or negative emotions. Everything was 'Eden' (delight). That was what God had planned for us, and that is what he is calling us back to. In fact, when one does a study of Mystical Theology, one comes across phrases suggesting this very scenario, the Catechism for example, calls the Holy Spirit, the 'Master of the Interior Life'. We can see there are indications of this interior possession of the soul by the power of the Holy Spirit.

The will was the domain of the Father. Again, this was God's original intention for the will which was lost because of original sin, but which God is restoring in this era in which you and I live. For our will to overflow with God, to be thoroughly immersed in the Divine Life, and indeed, for the Divine Will to become the animating principle of the soul, is what God intended so that the human will can be completely at rest and fulfilling its purpose, to enable the Divine Will to have its free operation in the soul.

Luisa teaches us how from the very first moment that Adam was conscious of his own existence, he knew of

God's love. She reveals to us Adam's experience of his being alive, and the first utterance he made when he opened his eyes…

"My daughter, I also feel the desire to share with you the first words pronounced on the lips of the first human being created by us. It behoves you to know that no sooner did Adam feel life, motion, and reason, than he beheld his God before him and understood that he had been formed by him. Adam felt within himself, within his whole being still fresh, the impressions of the touch of his Creator's creative hands. And in gratitude, in an impetus of love, he pronounced his first words…"

I love you my God, my Father, the Author of my life. [95]

It is to be noted that here we are, at the end of a particular phase of human history, the end of the era of the human will, and on the threshold of the reign of God's Divine Will, and we have had revealed to us all of these beautiful truths concerning the creation of the very first man, together with the very first words spoken by that very man. It is at times like this that we need to take to heart the dispositions of the Immaculate Heart of Mary, whose triumph this is, and make our hearts do as her heart did:

---

[95] Piccarreta, Luisa. Book of Heaven, Volume 33, December 10th, 1933.

'Mary treasured all these things, pondering them in her heart.'

Luke 2:19

Consequently, we must learn to treasure all that God is revealing to our souls, pondering them in our heart, so that the words that God is speaking to us can take root and find a place in us. Otherwise, there will be no fruit. Knowledge of this gift is priceless, but it needs to be able to take root in us.

Let us remember, all that God reveals to us about the creation, Adam, the gift of living in the Divine Will, it is all so that we can respond to God's call and become fully and completely the people that we were originally meant to be. It must be remembered that this beautiful gift is a restoration project, a call back to the origin, place and purpose for which God created us:

'Then they will rebuild the ancient ruins,
They will raise up the former devastations;
And they will repair the ruined cities,
The desolations of many generations.'
Isaiah 61:4

The beauty of how God created the first man and his plan and purpose for him, to fulfil the purpose of creation, is what we need to take to heart so that we can fully receive all that God wants to give us. Think of how God moulded

Adam, and then filled him with Trinitarian life, the Gift of Living in the Divine Will. With us, God is doing the 'operation' whilst we are active about our daily lives. He calls us to fully cooperate with his grace, rather than being like a statue on the floor.

This is a miracle of grace.

Fiat!

11. 'All Things Were Held in Common'

'All who believed were together and all things were held in common.'

Acts 2:44

This scripture comes immediately after the Church is born through the outpouring of the Holy Spirit, the first 3,000 or so converts are received, and the early community is being established. The power of the Holy Spirit took that first group of believers from independent ownership into what the Greeks called 'koinonia.' That is the Greek word for 'fellowship' and it refers to a deep unity in the heart, an inner unity whereby the soul desires to have a communal ownership of goods. It is quite foreign to the world in which we live whereby a person's goods are strictly their goods, not to be shared. Clearly this is an extreme viewpoint as many people are incredibly generous with their goods, possessions, finances, etc. However, it seems that there are also many for whom those goods are exclusively their own.

This is not the case in the Kingdom of the Divine Will. One of the wonderful graces given in the Divine Will is that all goods are mutually owned:

'Now the company of those who believed were of one heart and soul, and no one said that any of the things which he possessed was his own, but they had everything in common.'

Acts 4:32

The gift of Living in the Divine Will brings with it the graces of transtemporality, universality and multiplicity.[96] When a soul who lives in God's Divine Will performs an act, that soul is empowered by God to be present in all things by placing it in contact with all creatures of the past, present and future.[97] That is the grace of transtemporality. The word 'transtemporal' means to transcend time. Temporal pertains to the temporary world in which we find ourselves, whereas transcending that temporal world is a grace that God grants to the souls who live in His Will, with the associated goods that go with it. Thus, one act of mine in the Divine Will, can impact all creatures of the past, present and future. In other words, it is not exclusively my act, but it is owned by all because it is being done in God's Divine Will!

This grace of transtemporality disposes the soul for the grace of universality that exercises a universal sanctity in all things.[98] This means that whereas under normal circumstances when a soul does some act, or practices a

---

[96] Iannuzzi, Fr J., The Gift of Living in the Divine Will in the writings of Luisa Piccarreta, Missionaries of the Holy trinity, 2013. P.60.
[97] Ibid. P. 109
[98] Ibid.

virtue, or receives a sacrament, it is usually for that person's personal growth in sanctity. However, when a soul lives in the Divine Will, that growth in sanctity impacts all creatures of all times and produces a universal sanctification. Thus, the goods of the act are mutually owned by all creatures!

Finally, the graces of transtemporality and universality causes a diffusion and multiplication of its divine acts in all things.[99] So not only are all the acts impacting all creatures in all eras of humanity, and thus sanctifying all creatures of all time (because such acts transcend time), but those acts are multiplied to infinity because they are done not with the soul's own human will, but with God's Divine Will. Consider that when Jesus was on earth, his acts, all of which were done in the Divine Will, impacted all souls in just this way with these graces, because those acts were all done in the eternal mode of prayer and action. Jesus teaches Luisa of the soul living in the Divine Will, 'it can be said that she continues Our Life upon earth.'[100] In other words, every time the soul in the Divine Will performs an act following the teaching given by the Lord Jesus, His own Life is duplicated in the soul and that soul continues His Life as if he were present here and now.

Here is what Luisa has to say about all our acts being held in common:

---

[99] Ibid.

[100] Piccarreta, L., Book of Heaven, Volume 29, October 12th, 1931.

'Man is the new heavens, and more than the heavens above the earth, it can be said that each soul is an animated star. All that the first man Adam did, up to what the last one to come will do, was to be in common among them. Therefore, man was to possess not only his own strength, but the strength of all.' [101]

If we recall that the title of Luisa's writings is 'The call to the creature to the order, place and purpose for which they were created by God,' then recognise that God's purpose was for all goods to be held in common with all. However, the temptation can be to view this from the exterior life. Our houses, cars, income, savings, etc. These don't just belong to us, but to all. However, the greater goods are those of the interior life, the graces, virtues, crosses, etc. These goods are eternal and infinite when done in the Divine Will, and they impact all creatures of all times. So when a soul in the Divine Will has a day of fasting, that act has an impact which is trans-temporal, universal, and multiplied to infinity. Therefore, it is in common with all.

One act in My Will offers Me the acts of all souls, loves me for all and makes me perform the greatest excess of love and works for the good of souls. [102]

---

[101] Piccarreta, L., Book of Heaven, Volume 18, December 6th, 1925.

[102] Piccarreta, L., Book of Heaven, Volume 36, August 28th, 1938

First note that Jesus refers to just one act in His Will. One breath in His Will loves Him for all souls. These acts are not big, they are ordinary, normal, simple acts. The movements of the fingers, heartbeats, good thoughts, breaths, good words. Any good act can be elevated into the Divine Will by God's grace, and thus it becomes universally shared. That is the earthy perspective. What is the heavenly perspective? Well, the principle purpose of the Gift is to render unto God perfect glory on behalf of all humanity, past, present and future. We have a debt to God, all of humanity does. Fortunately, God has given us this beautiful gift so that the children of the Divine Will can pay that debt by rendering unto God the perfect glory of all time, for all, on behalf of all.

Again, Jesus declares to Luisa:

"All acts done in My Will diffuse everywhere, and all take part in them."[103]

The soul performing these acts generally cannot see them diffusing everywhere. We believe this is the case because the Word of Christ in Luisa's writings declares this to be so. We do the acts in faith, much like when we go to confession or communion, we receive the grace of the sacrament in faith.

---

[103] Piccarreta, L., Book of Heaven, Volume 18, November 22nd, 1925.

Arguably we do not 'feel' the sins leaving us when we confess, though we might get a little emotional. When the priest absolves us, there will probably be no sense experience. This is normal in the Christian life. It is demonstrated clearly in this reading from Luisa. One small act in the Divine Will immediately diffuses to every living soul on earth at this moment in time and to every soul all the way back to Adam, and forward in time to every soul until the last one that God will create. All souls take part in them, and God receives a perfect return of glory on behalf of every soul who takes part in any act in the Divine Will.

Jesus reminded Luisa that His work is His. He is the One who elevates the soul into the eternal mode of prayer and action which is the Gift of Living in the Divine Will. He is the One who has performed every act already and fuses said acts into our souls. He is the One who suffered, died, rose, ascended, so that we could receive this gift with all of the associated goods at this moment in time.

"In everything you do, I make you act on behalf of all souls, embrace all and make up for each of their acts in the name of all." [104]

This is what Jesus was doing on earth, and the task that He has entrusted to us. He desires that we should operate like Him at this moment in time because this was the way that all

[104] Piccarreta, L., Book of Heaven, Volume 17, June 3rd, 1923.

human creatures were meant to live from the very beginning. We were not made to be selfish, but to act as a human family, loving one another fully, acting on behalf of each other, and doing our divine acts for one another. When one soul on the other side of the planet does one act in the Divine Will, every soul should feel the impact of that act as if all were doing it. That hasn't happened in six thousand years with the exception of Jesus and Mary. Now, it is being restored.

By withdrawing from Our Divine Will man exited from within it, and his human acts that were once accomplished in Our Will remained as a pledge and a rightful claim for mankind. [105]

Jesus is referring to Adam when He talks about 'man exiting from within it.' Before Adam exited from the Divine Will all of his acts were performed in the eternal mode of prayer and action that is the Gift of Living in the Divine Will. These acts were not lost after the Fall, but rather they remain as a pledge and rightful claim for us all. What does this mean? A pledge can be defined as something given or held as security to guarantee payment of a debt or fulfilment of an obligation. Consequently, the acts Adam and Eve did before the Fall are held in the Divine Will as the fulfilment of an obligation. What is the obligation? The human creature was created for the glory of God and has an obligation to

---

[105] Piccarreta, L., Book of Heaven, Volume 29, June 30th, 1931.

love God for every moment of its existence. Adam's acts which were done before the Fall are held in the Divine Will in order to help us to fulfil that obligation.

The revelation that all acts were to be held in common amongst all of us is also something that flows from the life of the Trinity. Jesus taught Luisa:

'There are no curtains of secrets between this soul and US (The Trinity); there is no "Ours" and "yours", for everything is in common; and what We are by nature – impeccable, holy – we render the soul by grace, so that no disparity may exist between the soul and US.' [106]

Remember that 'everything is in common,' that there is no 'Ours' and 'yours.' The selfishness of the human race is entirely because of sin. Otherwise everything is held in common. What God is by nature, He wishes to render the soul by grace. This is most wonderfully seen in the Blessed Virgin Mary who lived a very quiet and hidden life when on earth, performing no public miracles and proclaiming no message of the gospel. Only after her Assumption into Heaven did she begin the miracles and proclaiming through a multitude of apparitions and locutions. However, between the soul in the Divine Will and the Trinity, Christ reveals that there are no 'curtains' of secrets. Perhaps the use of the word curtain needs explaining. In the Old Testament, the

---

[106] Piccarreta, L., Book of Heaven, Volume 11, March 17th, 1914.

book of Exodus, God instructs Moses about the building of a place of worship in the desert. This was called the Tabernacle. Catholics might think of the Blessed Sacrament Tabernacle, but this was very different. It was a tent but without a roof, rectangular in shape, with another tent inside it, and a further enclosure within that other tent. These had names, the Court of Sacrifice, the Holy Place, and the Holy of Holies. The Holy of Holies was separated from the Holy Place by a curtain, a thick veil. The same applied for the Holy Place, it was separated from the Court of Sacrifice by a thick veil – a curtain. The drawing back of the curtain reveals what is hidden behind, whether that is the Holy Place or Holy of Holies. The word to reveal, or revelation, in the New Testament is *apocalypse* and it comes from two words meaning 'to unveil' to make known what is hidden. This is what Jesus is doing with the writings on the Divine Will. He is making known that which has been hidden since the time of Adam. He is drawing back the curtain which hides the rich treasures of the Trinitarian life.

God wants the soul to be in fellowship with Him. The Greek word for fellowship is *koinonia*. It means to be in communion with, to share in common, intimacy. The gift of Living in the Divine Will is where God shares his very Will with the human creature so that we can participate more fully in the Trinitarian life with every single act that we do throughout the day or night. This gift enables us to have access to all of God's goods so that we can hold in common

God's own rich treasures. God wants us also to reciprocate this by recognising that every act we do in the Divine Will is to be held in common by all people of all time, past, present, and future. Nothing can be counted as 'mine,' but all is 'held in common.' This actually makes the soul richer because now that I share my own (spiritual) goods, I also gain access to all of the spiritual goods of all souls of all time. One becomes richer by sharing what one has.

"My daughter, listen to the admirable secret of my Volition. If the creature wants to find all that which has been done of beauty, of good, of sanctity, in the whole story of the world, by me, by the celestial Mama and by all the saints, she must enter in the Divine Will; in him one finds all in act. As you paid attention to every act, you remembered it, you offered it, thus the saint that had done that act, that sacrifice, felt himself called by the wayfaring soul and saw his act palpating anew on earth, hence the glory to his Creator and to himself is doubled, and you that offered it (are) covered with the celestial dew of the good of that holy act; and according to the noble and high purpose with which it became offered, thus more intense and great is the glory and good that it produces. How many riches my Will possesses! There are all my acts, those of the Sovereign Queen, that are all in expectation of being called, offered by the creature, in order to duplicate the good for the benefit of creatures and in order to give us double glory; they want to be remembered, called, in order to palpate as new life in the midst of creatures, but for lack of attention there are some who die, some who with difficulty through weakness, some who are numb for the cold, some who don't have anything to satiate their hunger. Our goods, acts and

sacrifices, don't depart if not called, because with remembering them and offering them [creatures] dispose themselves to recognize them and to receive the good that our acts contain. Then there is no greater honor that you can give to all Heaven, than to offer their acts that they did in earth, for the noble, most high and sublime purpose than that the Kingdom of the Divine Will comes upon the earth." [107]

Consider this in the light of human behaviours: Think about the way a person might write their biography, revealing to us the way they have lived certain aspects of their life. Clearly they can't include every detail of their life, so they are only going to reveal certain aspects depending on their motive for writing. The person reading gets insight into a celebrity, monarch, famous personality that they are interested in. The author writing their biography gets their message out, earns some money, and possibly answers some questions that have been raised about aspects of their life. Either way, the story has been shared and both parties benefit to a certain degree.

Contrast that with what Jesus reveals in the narrative above. The Church gives us the Saints and their writings (where they have them). By accessing the stories of these Saints, we can, in the Divine Will, make their acts our own, and then offer them back to God for His eternal glory and the glory of the Saint. As the act is called on by the person living in the Divine Will, the acts of the Saints palpitate on earth once again. They throb with life like a beating heart,

---

[107] Piccarreta, L., Book of Heaven, Volume 29, October 8th, 1931.

and the Saint can see their acts on earth once again. Consequently, the acts of all the Saints are in heaven awaiting the children of the Divine Will to call on them and enable them to palpitate on earth once again, to be offered back to God for His glory and that of His Saints.

Everything is to be held in common.

This does not just apply to the Saints, but also to all that God has done throughout human history:

"My daughter, all that has been done by Our Divinity, both in Creation and in Redemption, has not all been absorbed by the creature, but is all in my Divine Will, in waiting, to give itself to creatures. If you could see everything in my Divine Fiat, you would find an army of acts of Ours, which came out of Us to be given to creatures; but because Our Will does not reign, they have neither the space in which to put them, nor the capacity to receive them. And this divine militia has been waiting for as long as twenty centuries to place itself in office of exercise, so as to bring to creatures the gifts, the clothings, the joys and the divine weapons which each of Our acts possesses, in order to form together with them one single divine army – a celestial militia. Now, so that the Kingdom of Our Divine Will may reign in the midst of creatures, it is necessary that the creature absorb into herself all of these acts of the Divinity done for love of them and absorb them so much into herself, as to enclose within herself everything that my Fiat possesses, interiorizing them and consummating them within herself. So, my Divine Will, consummated within the creature, will make this whole divine army re-enter into her. All of Our acts which came out of Us for love of them, in Creation, Redemption and Sanctification, will reinter into creatures,

and my Divine Will, re-entered and consummated within them, will feel triumphant and will reign, dominant, together with Our divine army. This is why I do nothing but make you sip, continuously, everything that was done by Us and that is done in Creation, Redemption and Sanctification - so as to be able to say once again, as I did on the Cross: 'I have consummated everything – I have nothing left to do in order to redeem man.' So shall my Will repeat: 'I have consummated it in this creature, in a way that all Our acts have been enclosed in her - I have nothing left to add. I have consummated everything, so that man might be restored and the Kingdom of my Divine Will may have Its life and Its regime on earth as It does in Heaven." [108]

Fiat!

[108] Piccarreta, L., Book of Heaven, Volume 25, October 28th, 1928.

12. Luisa Piccarreta, The Little Daughter of the Divine Will

'Assuming that you have heard of the stewardship of God's grace that was given to me for you, how the mystery was made known to me by revelation.'

Ephesians 3:2, 3

I have placed this chapter on Luisa at the back of the book on purpose. Luisa wanted to be hidden, silent. So, I have hidden her silently at the back of this book, in her honour.

Saint Paul teaches us that he was made the steward of a grace that was meant for the Church in Ephesus. This is one of the ways that grace works. God can give us the grace that is intended for another, and we become the steward of that grace, until it is imparted on the soul for whom it is intended. For example, when a person gives a retreat to a group of individuals, the person giving the retreat, if they prepare correctly, is the steward of graces that God has deposited in their soul. As the retreat is given, the graces are imparted to those attending. I record here a moment of grace in Luisa's life that defined her:

When she was thirteen, while at home, Luisa heard a great uproar coming from the street, and she went out to the balcony to see what was happening.

A terrible vision appeared before her eyes: the street was crowded with shouting people, and with armed soldiers who, containing the crowd, were leading three prisoners. Among these, Luisa recognized Jesus, carrying the cross on His shoulders. Afflicted and terrorized, Luisa contemplated this sad procession, but when the Divine Convict was under her balcony, He raised His head and said: "Anima, aiutami!" ("Soul, help me!").

At this scene, Luisa cried out and lost her senses.

This extraordinary event marked for Luisa a decisive turning point in her life, because on that day she accepted her state of victim of expiation for the sins of men.[109]

Luisa Piccarreta is the head of a mission, appointed by the Lord Jesus Christ, and with all of the grace for that mission deposited in her soul ready to be imparted to all the souls who will come under that mission. Her title, given by Christ, is 'Little daughter of the Divine Will.' Visitors to her home town of Corato who go to her tomb will see this title written in Italian by her tomb.

---

[109] https://www.servantofgodluisapiccarreta.com/biography

Luisa was born in Corato, Italy, on the morning of April 23, 1865. It was the first Sunday after Easter, which is now known as Divine Mercy Sunday. She was baptised in the evening of that same day in the Mother Church. Her father, a farmer, managed the land of a rich landlord. During the summer he moved with his family to a farm in the Murge plateau. Luisa attended the first years of primary school with the Sisters. As a child, she preferred to stay alone for a long time to immerse herself in long meditations and prayers.

However, her life took a decisive turning point at the age of about 16, when there was a mysterious state of suffering which confined her to bed and left her in a state of loss of consciousness. Despite medical treatment, it was clear that only the blessing of a priest enabled her to come out of her 'usual state.' Luisa offered her suffering for the benefit of humanity accepting until her death the complete confinement to bed that lasted about 70 years.

Her particular condition convinced the Archbishop of Trani to entrust her permanently to the spiritual care of a priest. Of fundamental importance was the contribution of Fr Gennaro De Gennaro. After having heard what happened to her during her states of loss of consciousness, he gave her the 'obedience' to write the 'diary,' a task to which Luisa would remain faithful, albeit with great reluctance, writing about 10,000 pages from February 28th, 1899, to December 28th, 1938. The main theme is "The Gift of Living in the Divine Will".

Her daily life did not appear to be extraordinary. She supported herself with her work of embroidery on the 'bombolo,' and, with her sister Angelian who looked after her, she welcomed girls who wanted to learn that art. She was allowed to attend Mass at home. However, her constant attitude of concealment didn't reduce her fame, attracting priests and lay people from all over, even arousing some discontent.

Luisa survived on the Eucharist. She was required to eat a small dish of grapes by order of obedience, but once they had been eaten, she would bring them back up, whole, intact, complete. Consequently, her only nourishment was the Eucharist and the Divine Will.

However, every night her body would become like a marble statue and she would bilocate with Jesus around the world, the universe, heaven, purgatory and hell. The next morning the priest would bring her out of this state by making a simple sign of the cross anywhere on her body. She also had regular heavenly visitations from Jesus and Mary. She suffered the invisible stigmata, plus the crown of thorns was regularly placed on her head, all of which she suffered quietly and hiddenly, only recording the events in her diaries because of holy obedience.

In photos of Luisa she is often seen sitting upright in her bed. This is how she was for the entire time she was confined to bed according to the Will of God. She did not lean back on the pillows that are seen, but sat forward, gazing at her cross, writing in her diaries, doing her work. Indeed, when she died on March 4th 1947, she could not be laid flat in accordance with the usual burial custom. Her many years of sitting up had caused the bones in her spine to fuse, so she died sitting up, and she is buried sitting up. This is evidence in photos of her funeral whereby the coffin has a glass portion and Luisa can be seen.

Father Benedetto Calvi describes what happened in the captions of some photographs in his photograph collection:

'Her whole body did not develop rigor mortis, which happens to all human bodies right after death. People could see it every day she was viewed, before the eyes of the people of Corato and so many people from other towns, who came to Corato just to be able to see and touch with their own hands this unique and extraordinary case: to be able to move her head in every direction with no effort at all; to raise her arms, bend them, bend her hands and all the fingers. Even her eyelids could be lifted and her eyes could be seen bright as before without the film of death. Luisa seemed to be alive, as if she were sleeping.' [110]

A group of doctors had gathered to confirm that Luisa had died.

---

110 Del Genio, Maria R., The Sun of My Will, Libreria Edirice Libreria Edirice Vaticana. Page 179.

Also, in the register at the House of the Daughters of Divine Zeal it is written:

'With the body prepared, adorned with flowers and lights, it was exposed for public veneration to which a great crowd hastened, even from nearby towns, in order to see one last time the Saint, which was what they called her. It was the wish of her sister Angelina that our Sisters took turns placing sacred objects on the blessed remains. During the three days that she [Luisa] was exposed, the Lord showed that this soul was not just a simple creature, but a holy victim. Her body is flexible, everyone can see that even her blood is circulating in her veins' [111]

Luisa is in the process of Canonisation at the time of writing, her current status as at the time of publication is 'Servant of God,'

Many souls ask me why Luisa? One needs to review salvation history for an answer. God chose Adam as the first man; Noah to save the world via the ark; Abraham as the Father of all believers; Joseph as the patriarch who would store the grain in Egypt; Moses was chosen as the liberator of Israel from Egypt and the Law Giver; Joshua was chosen as the man who would lead Israel in its conquest of the Holy Land; David chosen as the greatest King in Israel; Solomon chosen as the wisest; Isaiah chosen as a prophet, as were

---

[111] Ibid., page 180

Jeremiah, Ezekiel, Amos, Samuel and others. Then we have John the Baptist as the last of the Prophets, Our Lady as the Mother of God, Peter as the Prince of Apostles, Paul as the Apostle to the Gentiles, John chosen as custodian of the Mother of God, St Joseph chosen as her spouse and guardian of the Son of God. Then a long and growing army of Saints, all chosen by God for particular tasks.

So instead of saying 'why Luisa?', consider your own calling. God has called you to give your fiat to the gift of living in the Divine Will. God wants to raise you to the heights of holiness, with Luisa as one of many intercessors in heaven praying for you and guiding you through this life.

'Therefore, since we are surrounded by so great a cloud of witnesses, let us also lay aside every weight, and sin which clings so closely, and let us run with perseverance the race that is set before us.'

Hebrews 12:1

You are like an athlete in a stadium running a race, fighting a good fight, competing for a prize which will never spoil or fade. God wants to enrich you with graces beyond your imagination, and there is an army of Saints willing you on and praying for you to receive these graces.

'Now to him who by the power at work within us is able to do far more abundantly than all that we ask or imagine.'

Ephesians 3:20

Luisa is the herald of the Divine Will, the first soul born in a state of Original Sin that God has raised to the heights of holiness, the state of beatitude whilst on earth. He has given her possession of the Divine Will and immeasurable graces. She is the first. She wrote her diaries so that you could follow, but walking your own unique path along this route. On this journey, God can do far more abundantly than you can either ask or imagine, which is why you need to read, learn, listen, contemplate, be silent, and receive all that God wants to give you. This is what Luisa did. She was empty and God filled her. She had a poor education, but God gave her the richest theology in the history of the Church, teaching her about the interior life of God and Our Lady. Now this is passed to you so that you can fulfil the journey that God is calling you to walk, and Luisa has picked you out to walk this path.

'God has created me to do Him some definite service. He has committed some work to me which He has not committed to another. I have my mission. I may never know it in this life, but I shall be told it in the next. I am a link in a chain, a bond of connection between persons.

He has not created me for naught. I shall do good; I shall do His work. I shall be an angel of peace, a preacher of truth in my own place, while not intending it if I do but keep His commandments.

Therefore, I will trust Him, whatever I am, I can never be thrown away. If I am in sickness, my sickness may serve Him, in perplexity, my perplexity may serve Him. If I am in sorrow, my sorrow may serve Him. He does nothing in vain. He knows what He is about. He may take away my friends. He may throw me among strangers. He may make me feel desolate, make my spirits sink, hide my future from me. Still, He knows what He is about.'

St John Henry Cardinal Newman

Luisa's writings

Her diaries on the gift of living in the Divine Will are her personal journals containing her locutions from Jesus, with some from Mary, teaching us about this gift and how to live in it. These diaries number 36 volumes.

She also wrote the *Hours of the Passion* which reveals the last 24 hours of Christ's life on earth. These teach the soul about the interior sufferings of Christ as he suffered for the sins of the world and made perfect reparation to the Father. These are powerful meditations that can sanctify the soul and help it to grow in the Divine Will. They were revealed by the Lord Jesus Christ.

The Blessed Virgin Mary in the Kingdom of the Divine Will were teachings from Our Lady given to Luisa who faithfully wrote them down. They comprise of 36 lessons, corresponding to the 36 volumes from Christ. Our Lady teaches about her own interior life and encourages the soul to take hold of this beautiful gift promising us her help. This is a treasure. Our Lady calls it 'gold.'

Luisa also wrote her "Childhood memories," "*The pilgrimage of the Soul in the Divine Will*," "*The Three Appeals*," her letters, and "*The Rounds of the Soul in the Divine Will*."

All of these writings can be obtained from various outlets.

Servant of God, Luisa Piccarreta, pray for us.

Fiat!

13. Prayers in the Divine Will

'Behold, I am standing by the spring of water;

Pray give me a … drink,'

Genesis 24:43

The Prevenient act is to be said at the start of the day.

The Morning Offering Prayer in the Divine Will

(The "Prevenient Act")[112]

O Immaculate Heart of Mary, Mother and Queen of the Divine Will, I entreat you, by the infinite merits of the Sacred Heart of Jesus, and by the graces God has granted to you since your Immaculate Conception, the grace of never going astray.

Most Sacred Heart of Jesus, I am a poor and unworthy sinner, and I beg of You the grace to allow our mother Mary and Luisa to form in me the divine acts You purchased for

[112] Piccarreta, L., Divine Will Prayer Book, Missionaries of the Holy Trinity, translated by Rev. Joseph Iannuzzi. P. 65 (Date of publication not given).

me and for everyone. These acts are the most precious of all, for they carry the Eternal Power of your Fiat and they await my "Yes, your Will be done" (Fiat Voluntas Tua). So I implore you, Jesus, Mary and Luisa to accompany me as I now pray:

I am nothing and God is all, come Divine Will. Come Heavenly Father to beat in my heart and move in my Will; come beloved Son to flow in my Blood and think in my intellect; come Holy Spirit to breathe in my lungs and recall in my memory.

I fuse myself in the Divine Will and place my I love You, I adore You and I bless You God in the Fiats of creation. With my I love You my soul bilocates in the creations of the heavens and the earth: I love You in the stars, in the sun, in the moon and in the skies; I love You in the earth, in the waters and in every living creature my Father created out of love for me, so that I may return love for love.

I now enter into Jesus' Most Holy Humanity that embraces all acts. I place my I adore You Jesus in your every breath, heartbeat, thought, word and step. I adore You in the sermons of your public life, in the miracles You performed, in the Sacraments You instituted and in the most intimate fibres of your Heart.

I bless You Jesus in your every tear, blow, wound, thorn and in each drop of Blood that unleashed light for the life of every human. I bless You in all your prayers, reparations, offerings, and in each of the interior acts and sorrows You suffered up to your last breath on the Cross. I enclose your life and all your acts, Jesus, within my I love You, I adore You and I bless You.

I now enter into the acts of my mother Mary and of Luisa. I place my I thank you in Mary and Luisa's every thought, word and action. I thank you in the embraced joys and sorrows in the work of Redemption and Sanctification. Fused in your acts I make my I thank You and I bless You God flow in the relations of every creature to fill their acts with light and life: To fill the acts of Adam and Eve; of the patriarchs and prophets; of souls of the past, present and future; of the holy souls in purgatory; of the holy angels and saints.

I now make these acts my own, and I offer them to You, my tender and loving Father. May they increase the glory of your children, and may they glorify, satisfy and honour You on their behalf.

Let us now begin our day with our divine acts fused together. Thank You Most Holy Trinity for enabling me to enter into union with You by means of prayer. May your Kingdom come, and your will be done on earth as it is in heaven.

Fiat!

A shorter prevenient act:

O Jesus, in You, with You, and for You, through, with and in the Immaculate Heart of Mary – Your Mother and my mother – I consecrate and give my will to You in exchange for Your Divine Will. I truly want Your Divine Will to generate its Divine Life in me this day – to think in all my thoughts, to speak in all my words and operate in all my actions, for the glory of our Heavenly Father and to fulfil the purpose of Creation.

I fuse my human will with Your Divine Will, to flow with you everywhere, to do with you what you do and fulfil the role that You desire of me as Your child and divine companion.

Abandoned in Your arms, my Jesus, I invite all the angels and Saints, especially Mary, Most Holy, to join in all that the Divine Will does in me today. I am confident that You will not fail to give me the grace to be always faithful and attentive to Your action within me, so that my own will dare not interfere with Your freedom to form Your Real Life in me.

O my Jesus, I love you with Your own Will and thank you profoundly for the knowledge and Gift of the Divine Will. Amen.[113]

Fiat!

---

[113] By Thomas M. Fahy who introduced me to this beautiful gift at Garabandal, 2010.

Prayer for Luisa's beatification

O Most Holy Trinity, Our Lord Jesus Christ taught us that as we pray we should ask that our Father's Name be always glorified, that His Will be done on earth and that His Kingdom should come to reign among us.

In our great desire to make known this Kingdom of love, justice and peace, we humbly ask that you glorify your Servant Luisa, the Little Daughter of the Divine Will who, with her constant prayer and suffering, deeply yearned for the salvation of souls and the coming of God's Kingdom in the world.

Following her example we pray to You, Father, Son and Holy Spirit, to help us joyously embrace the crosses of this world so that we may also glorify your Name and enter into the Kingdom of Your Will. Amen.

+Archbishop Carmelo Cassati, Archdiocese of Trani-Nazareth, Italy.

Fiat!

Consecration to the Divine Will [114]

O Adorable and Divine Will, here I am, before the Immensity of Your Light, that Your Eternal Goodness may open to me the doors, and make me enter into it, to form my life all in You Divine Will.

Therefore, prostrate before Your Light, I, the littlest among all creatures, come, O Adorable Will, into the little group of the First Children of Your Supreme Fiat. Prostrate in my nothingness, I beseech and implore Your Endless Light, that it may want to invest me and eclipse everything that does not belong to You, in such a way that I may do nothing other than look, comprehend, and live in You, Divine Will.

It shall be my Life, the Centre of my intelligence, the Enrapture of my heart and of my whole being. In this heart the human will shall no longer have life; I shall banish it forever, and shall form the New Eden of Peace, of Happiness, and of Love. With it I shall always be happy; I shall have a Unique Strength, and a Sanctity that Sanctifies everything and brings everything to God.

Here prostrate, I invoke the Help of the Sacrosanct Trinity, that They admit me to Live in the Cloister of the Divine Will, so as to restore in me the Original Order of Creation, just as the creature was Created.

---

[114] +Archbishop Glovan Battista Pichierri of Trani-Barletta-Bisceglie and Nazareth.

Celestial Mother, Sovereign Queen of the Divine Fiat, take me by the hand and enclose me in the Light of the Divine Will. You shall be my Guide, my tender Mother; You shall guard Your child, and shall teach me to live and to maintain myself in the Order and in the Bounds of the Divine Will. Celestial Sovereign, to Your Immaculate Heart I entrust my whole being; I shall be the tiny little child of the Divine Will. You shall teach me the Divine Will, and I shall be attentive in listening to You. You shall lay Your Blue Mantle over me, so that the infernal serpent may not dare to penetrate into this Sacred Eden to entice me and make me fall into the maze of the human will.

Heart of my Highest Good, Jesus, You shall give me Your Flames, that they may burn me, consume me, nourish me, to form in me the Life of the Supreme Will.

Saint Joseph, You shall be my Protector, the Custodian of my heart, and shall keep the keys of my will in Your hands. You shall keep my heart jealously, and shall never give it to me again, that I may be sure never to go out of the Will of God.

Guardian Angel, guard me, defend me, help me in everything, so that my Eden may grow flourishing and be the call of the whole world into the Will of God.

Celestial Court, come to my help, and I promise you to live always in the Divine Will.

Amen.

BIBLIOGRAPHY

All scripture quotations, unless otherwise indicated, are taken from the website **www.blueletterbible.org**.

I have used either the NASB2020, or Revised Standard Version.

The New American Bible. Oxford: Oxford University Press. 1990.

My preferred version of the Bible for study is:

The Didache Bible, Revised Standard Version. Midwest Theological Forum, Inc., IL. 2015.

Whenever I have referred to the original Hebrew or Greek translations of the Bible I have used the resource on www.blueletterbible.org who have taken the information from:-

STRONG, James, S.T.D., L.L.D. *Strong's Exhaustive Concordance of the Bible.* World

Bible Publishers, Iowa Falls, Ia. 1993.

Catechism of the Catholic Church, London: Geoffrey Chapman, 1994. Abbreviated as CCC.

Iannuzzi, Fr J. Ph.B, STV, M.Div., STL, STD, *The Gift of Living in the Divine Will in the Writings of Luisa Piccarreta.* Missionaries of the Holy Trinity, Inc. 2013.

Piccarreta, Luisa, *The Kingdom of the Divine Will in the Midst of the Creatures, Book of Heaven, The call to the creatures to the order, to the place and to the purpose for which they were created by God.* No publisher details given, nor date of publication. Only a note that this is a New Limited Edition available until the Church publishes its official translation.

Cited as '*Book of Heaven*'.

Piccarreta, Luisa, *The Blessed Virgin Mary in the Kingdom of the Divine Will,* Missionaries of the Holy Trinity, Inc.

* 9 7 8 1 0 6 8 7 7 3 9 3 8 *
WS - #0114 - 191224 - C0 - 210/148/10 - PB - 9781068773938 - Gloss Lamination